THE SIMPLEST BOOK FOR TECHNICAL ANALYSIS

MUKUL AGRAWAL

Published By

Invincible Publishers

Published by

Invincible Publishers
201A, SAS Tower, Sector 38, Gurugram – 122003
Phone: +91-124-4034247, +91 9599066061
www.invinciblepublishers.com

Sales: Office No. 109 Prakash Mahal Ansari Road Daryaganj,
Near ICICI Bank - 110002
Phone: +91-11-40198405
Email: invinciblepublishers@gmail.com

First edition – 2022

ISBN: 978-93-94200-49-4

Printed at Nutech Print Services - India

Contents

Let's Understand the Analysis First:

It's human nature; whenever we have to take any decision related to anything in every stage of life; we do analysis. Let's try to connect from your life: In childhood, your parents must have made some decision for you like: which city is best for you, which school is best for you, as you grow you also got the right to made the decision for yourself like, which subject you like to go with for your future, which city you prefer to live and work, and one of the most crucial decisions of your life might be to whom you will get married! Right?

As we go through our life cycle, we make many decisions.

What do you think is the main factor that is crucial to making better decisions?

Well! The answer is **Analysis**.

Before making any decision, we analyze the factors involved in decision-making.

Here Analysis means nothing but Inspection/ Scanning/ Examination; say whatever you feel good about.

The meaning remains the same. You want to know the about,

features, specifications, pros, and cons of something about which you have to decide whether it is suitable for you or not?

These are nothing but just a factor that everyone considers in the decision-making process.

I hope till now, you must get the point of what Analysis is all about.

Analysis plays a crucial role in life because I believe life is all about decision- making, and to make a decision, you should know the factors behind the scene.

"Whenever you see a successful business, someone once made a courageous decision."
— Peter F. Drucker

Likewise, we use the same analysis concept in Finance also.

Whenever we need to make any financial decision, whether it is earning, investing, or spending, we must go through an analysis process.

As I always used to share this in my videos that "pehle jaano, samjho phir financial decision lo."

In this book, you will get in-depth knowledge of technical Analysis. And when I say in-depth, I mean it.

From the Introduction to technical Analysis to how to trade with the help of technical Analysis, this book will work as a guide

for you.
You will feel like Mr. Mukul Agrawal is holding my hand in this journey of Technical Analysis.

So, Let's get started.

Let's decode Technical Analysis.

We will use TA as a short form of Technical Analysis in the further journey.

By Definition mentioned on the internet, "Technical analysis is a trading discipline employed to evaluate investments and identify trading opportunities by analyzing statistical trends gathered from trading activity, such as price movement and volume." Posted on Investopedia.

But you are with me, and we don't believe in theories, right? So, we will understand Technical Analysis in our own way!

Anything available in this universe has a value, or we may say that it has a price (Har chij ki keemat hoti h bhaiyo or behno).

You must have heard from your parents about the price fluctuation of vegetables asper the seasons and fruits as per seasons or events.

This fluctuation of Price is termed or called Price Action. Price is moving Up, Down, and sometimes No Change because of seasons, events, demand, supply, and many other factors which may affect the price of these commodities.

Analysis of this movement of Price is what we call "Technical Analysis."

When we say Price Analysis, it means we are Inspecting or Examining when the Price will go UP or Down, or No change. This includes the Price of past, present, and future predictions.

"Price phley kya tha? Av kya hai? Ar aagey kya rehne ka anumaan h?

"The study of just these three concepts is all about Technical Analysis. We will dig deeper into these three concepts step by step.

" Technical Analysis is the analysis of the price movement with respect to the price and time of any securities."

Technical Analysis (TA) VS Fundamental Analysis(-FA)

What is this new concept in between the journey of Technical Analysis?

Why are we comparing these two?

Let me answer these questions for you!

When we talk about Analysis, there are two brothers about whom we should know.

Although this is a TA book, to understand TA better, we also need to know how it is better than his brother (FA)? and the difference between them.

Don't worry; I won't take much of your time to Explain FA.

As we know, the study of price movement is known as Technical Analysis.

Likewise, when we study the core concept of anything, which helps us get the real value of the security, that is Fundamental Analysis.

As I explained earlier, the Analysis of price fluctuation of commodities(Vegetables or fruits), likewise when we talk about the Analysis of quality of commodities(Vegetables or foods), is known as Fundamental Analysis.

Kya buy krna h depends on Quality (Fundamental Analysis)

Kis price pe buy krna h depends on Price Movement (Technical Analysis) The same techniques work in Financial Market.

To analyze the quality of stocks, we do Fundamental Analysis.

To analyze the Price Movement of stocks, we do Technical Analysis.

That's it.

Now, you know about the two brothers of Analysis.

Let's restart the journey of Technical Analysis.

We live in a world full of Assumptions!

As we discussed decision-making earlier. You will relate that our decisions are more often based on Assumptions. While choosing the best school for our kids, we assume that Teachers must be good because fees are high. When something is expensive, we assume that it must be of good quality.

Likewise, when we study any topic, there will be some assumptions that the Inventor of that topic creates.

That's why we have the assumption of Technical Analysis also.

We will discuss each assumption step by step.

Assumptions of the Technical Analysis

You will get these assumptions everywhere on the internet, but the way of explanation is what makes us different from others.

Market Discounts everything: To understand this, we need to highlight one more topic called "Market Participants." They are people involved in the market. Who are they? You, yes, you read it right. Everyone involved in trading in the market is called a market participant. You, Me, or anyone who is buying or selling shares in the stock market. We all are participating in the market. Hence, we are called market participants.

Market Participants are further classified into different groups based on their turnover value.

FII(Foreign Institutional Investors): The one who stays out of the country and invests in our country's companies.

DII(Domestic Institutional Investors): The big fund houses of our country like LIC, UTI, HDFC AMC, ICICI AMC, and many more.

Ultra High Networth Individuals: They are the ones who have more than Rs. 25 Crores of Income.

Very High Networth Individuals: They are the ones who have an income in the range of Rs. 5 to 15 Crores

HNI (High Networth Individuals): They are the ones who have an income of Rs. 5 Crores

These data are based on Business Standard Article:

https://www.business-standard.com/about/who-is-high-net-worth-individuals#collapse

Retail Investors: As per the Business Standard article whose link I have attached above, the ones whose income is less than Rs. 5 Crores are considered retail investors.

As you can see earlier, I said we all are market participants.

It means every class of people involved in the stock trading activity.

You must agree with me that the one with more money must

have more sources of information about the market and stocks. And they get the information much before the retail investors. And as a human, we have the nature to act or react to news and events.

Let's imagine a situation you have invested a big sensible amount in a company. As one of the significant shareholders, you will get information about the company much before it reaches retail investors. If something wrong happens in the company, You must try to sell or book profit, and this action will lead to a decline in share price. On the other hand, If there is some good news about the company, you must start adding more shares to your portfolio, which will lead to a rise in price.

I hope everything is clear till now.

So, this is the base of the assumption of the Market discounts everything.

Any news related to the market or specific stocks comes into the market, and there is someone who reacts to that, which leads to a change in the price of the market.

There is a saying that the Market gives premiums and discounts on everything.

You must have noticed the rise in the price of the stock before the announcement of the result.

Fall in the price of the stock before any bad news hits the market.

What do you think about why these things happen?

I am repeating the line. We are the market participants. We make the price move in any direction. Some of us got the news faster, so we reacted and led to the price change.

Hence, the market discounts everything.

History Tends to repeat: This assumption is very clear and to the point. Technical Analyst believes that what happened in the past must repeat in the future because movement in price action involves a human who runs on emotions(Fear and Greed). Have you ever noticed that there is a point where stock prices always tend to hit and move?

You must have seen this. We call these points support and resistance. We will learn about this topic also in further chapters.

Because of this human behavior, prices tend to move in similar patter many times, which verifies the assumption that history tends to repeat.

The market moves in Trend: Experts believe that the market or price of stocks moves in a trend until there is some reason to change or stop the trend. The reason could be bad financial results, political issues, global issues, governance issues, profit booking, etc.

Until then market or stock price moves in a trend. Or you may say in a direction. Traders formed many directional trading strategies under this assumption.

It is quite easy to understand the logic behind this assumption is that if stock price gave a breakout and rose like a rocket, it further attracted other traders and investors too. This means more and more stock buying will come, leading the price towards a higher high. In that case, what will stop the price from rising? It might be some profit booking, bad news, or events related to the market and stocks. Until then, the market may move in the same direction we call a trend.

HAVE YOU EVER HEARD THE STORY OF "MOUNTAINEER"?

They are the one who tries to climb the mountain.

So, before starting the journey, they need to understand a few sets of rules and terms and conditions, or you can also say that the basic concept which will be useful to them in the process of mountain climbing. Those concepts will help them understand the journey much better, which further leads them toward success.

If I summarize this in a line," To climb the mountain, you should know the basics of How to climb the mountain." Right!?

The same concept works in the financial world also. To climb the mountain of TA, you should have a strong base of Technical Analysis, and you must know the basic concepts which will be used in the whole journey of this book.

High

Basic Concept of TA

As we all know now, "TA is all about the study of price movement with reference to the time."

One basic question you should ask is what led the price to move UP, Down or Flat?

I know you must have thought about this!

No worries, I am here for you to explain each and every point. Ever heard the term "Demand & Supply"? Let's try to understand!

Let's assume you have a car showroom on; one day, you saw your salesman struggling with two customers. Curiously, you stepped out of your cabin to understand the situation.

You: What is happening here? What is the problem?

Sales Man: Sir, they both want to buy the same car, but we have only a single piece left, and none of them agree to select any other car!

Here is a question for you, my friend, what will you do? Take a second to think. Well, in me, the best you can do is to increase the price of the car so that the one who wants to buy this car anyhow will pay a higher price for the car.

If you have any other better ideas for this situation, you can easily share them with me through any medium on social media.

Now, let's continue with our story and try to understand what actually happened in this situation.

Supply of a Car was 1(You had only one car of that model left in your showroom) The demand for a Car was 2(Two people are ready to buy the same car)

What this situation leads to?

This situation leads the price of the car higher. As I suggested, the situation is to raise the price of the and those who want to buy the car anyhow can pay the higher price.

This is what happens in the market on a daily basis.

Market participants are available to buy and sell; when buyers are more, the price moves UP; when sellers are more price moves Down, and when both are equal No change in price.

This is the whole base of TA.

Everything which you study in TA will roam around this concept only.

Now, let's talk about a few concepts that concepts which is necessary to understand the TA and also help in the analysis part in a further chapter.

Dow Theory

It's our Indian tradition that the Son will get the title of father. Likewise, the one who invents the theory or the one who first introduced the theory is called the father of that theory, and his/her title becomes the name of that theory.

The same happened with the "Dow Theory" Charles H. Dow(1851 – 1902) wrote his 255th editorial, "The Wall Street Journal," on the same editorial he introduced the "Dow Theory."

You must have gone through the many theories in your school/college life. Like: Newton's Law, Bernoulli's Law and Golden rule of commerce, etc., all these laws have their set of concepts or rules which needs to be followed in order to justify these laws. Ok, I don't discuss these laws.

What I am trying to say is that, like all these laws, "Dow Theory" also has some set of concepts that we need to check or follow in order to justify the Dow Theory.

Figure 1

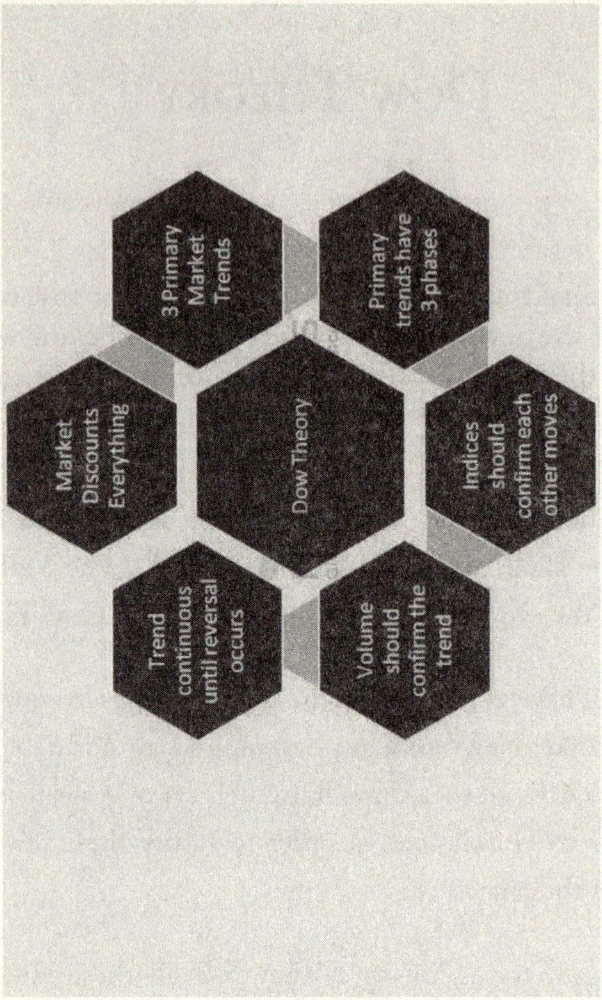

Dow Theory works like a road map or you can also say the guide of trading. What did Dow state?

Dow states that the Stock market is the barometer of the economy. It shows the whole business condition in the economy. He has never stated this theory as a guide for trading or investing, but he then believed that the stock market is the mirror of the whole economy. We can measure the performance of the market to get a view of the Primary trend of the market and also the trend of the stocks.

Why did he consider the stock market as a barometer of the economy? Let's think logically about which companies are listed in the stock market.

Companies of every sector, industry and type are listed in the stock market.

These companies are part of the economy; they invest, earn, and spend in the same economy. This further leads to money circulation within the economy, which leads to increase purchasing power.

More money

More expense

More production

More money

Cycle continues and all this can be observed in Stock Market.

So, this is what Dow believed.

But after his death in the year 1902, His associate "William P. Hamilton," who was also an editor of Dow's journal, continued the Dow theory; it took 27 years to organize and summarize the concepts of Dow as a Dow Theory which we are studying nowadays.

Now let's talk about the 6 Principles of Dow Theory which are mentioned in figure 1.

1. Market discounts everything: Do you remember one of the assumptions we talked about, "Market discounts everything"? The same concepts work here also. Dow theory states that the market incorporates every information available in the market. And so, the price reacts accordingly.

3 Market Trend: Dow Theory states that there are three trends available in themarket.

- **Primary Trend:** This is the longest trend, which lasts over 1 or 2 years. This might be a Bullish or Bearish Trend. This occurs because of the fundamentals of the market or any stock which lay the market participants keep on buying and maintaining the trend or vice-versa.

- **Secondary Trend:** In continuous Primary Trend, this lasts over a few weeks to a few months. A secondary trend is like a correction trend, or we can also say a pullback in the primary trend. This is the phase where investors/ traders book some profit or sometimes any short-term event occurs, which leads the market to a pullback phase. But most of the time, this act as a new entry zone for those who missed starting rally; they can enter at this level or vice-versa.

- **Minor Trend:** This trend last over a few days or weeks. This is considered as a noise of the market. Small correction or pullback happens in this trend under the secondary trend. Investors generally avoid this trend because sometime this disturbs the discipline of the investment.

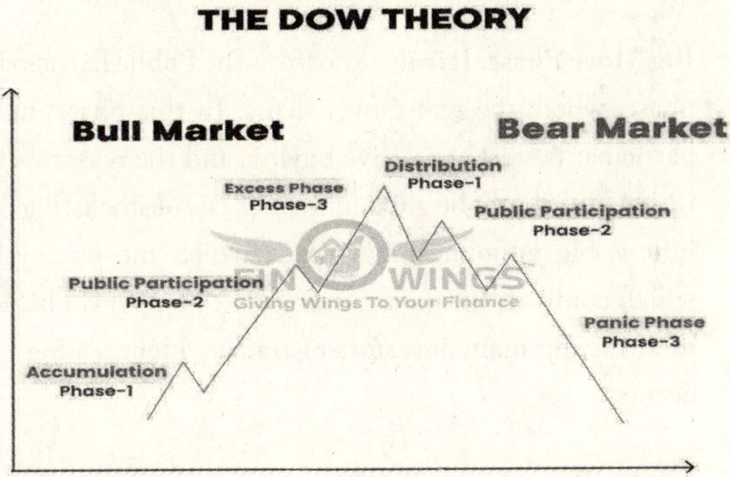

3 Phase of Primary trends: As I said earlier Primary Trend is a long-term trend that lasts over 1 or 2 years. This long trend needs to have some supportive structure to maintain its strength. That structure is defined in terms of phases.

- **In the Booming period or Bull Run:** The primary trend passes through 3 phases:

1. **Accumulation Phase:** As the word speaks for itself, Accumulation- Is the phase where market participants accumulate/collect the shares on the basis of the assumption that this company may do well in the future. This kind of assumption is based on the Fundamental analysis of the

stock, which you can learn from my course later. In this phase, the market may show confusion in direction. Market trades in a range. Generally, big players are involved during the accumulation phase.

2. **Big Move Phase:** It is also known as the Public Participation phase, where the real move occurs. In this phase, market participants start aggressive buying, and the reason behind this buying might be good fundamentals of stocks, big order inflow, big announcements, etc., which means anything which confirms the good future of the company. This leads to attracting many investors or traders. Hence, a big move occurs.

3. **Excess Phase:** Everything has its real value. Nothing can go till infinity. Right? So, the price of stocks, too, cannot move to infinity. No matter how good the company is performing. There must be a real value of the company, which justifies its value. In the booming phase, market participants just keep buying and buying without considering the real value of the stock or company. But in reality, it won't work for long. The big market participants are those who have little more knowledge about the market and the company. They prefer to value the market as per intrinsic value or real value. So, whatever they buy during a bull run, they use to sell at some particular time when they feel that the stock is not trading over its real value. This action leads to the Excess phase. The word itself speaks, Excess- Ab aur upr nhi jana h. I always use to discuss in my videos, always value the

real value. In the long run, only real value will sustain. The bubble will burst.

- **In Down Trend or Bear Run:** Like in a bull run, the Primary trend passes through 3 phases:

1. **Distribution Phase:** Just after the Excess phase, the distribution phase starts. In this phase, bulls (buyers of the market) start selling the share in parts, which seems like bulls distributing some shares to others; rallies paused at this phase. Like- the Accumulation phase in the Distribution phase also price moves in range.

2. **Big Move Phase:** Like in a bull run, a big move comes in a downtrend also, when market participants find something fishy in the market or particular stock. They want to protect their profit by selling their majority stakes.

3. **Despair Phase:** You can call it a Panic phase also because, in this phase, market participants start selling their holdings aggressively. The reason behind this panic selling might be some indication of big bad news like government change, company fraud, or natural disasters which affect the companies or economies. That fishy doubt which triggers a big move in a downtrend might get confirmed, which further leads to the panic phase.

- Indices should confirm each other moves: If two brothers of the same family study in the same school, and if both of them scored above 99%, then only we can say that the school is a good school. If one of them scored 99% and the other one scored 80%, it means school is not good. What am I doing? Please, this is not my thought process. This is what Dow's theory says.

If one index is performing, then the other index should also perform then; only the trend will get confirmed.

Actually, let's break the things to understand better.

Dow and his associate introduced two Indices (You can call them a brother Index).

1. **Dow Jones Industrial Average (DJIA):** It is nothing but the collection of 30 Blue-chip stocks in the U.S. Its Price is derived from the weighted average price of 30 Blue-chip companies in the United States. You can say it's a sense of U.S. Charles Dow created this index in 1896 as an attorney for the U.S economy.

2. **Dow Jones Transportation Average (DJTA):** It is the collection of 20 transport companies in the U.S. Its Price is derived from the weighted average price of the 20 traded transportation stocks in the U.S. Like in India, we have Bank Nifty, in which only banking stocks are grouped. The same happens in DJTA. In fact, it is the oldest stock index, founded in 1884 by Charles Dow.

So, now after you meet with the index brothers, let's discuss their relationship asper Dow theory.

As I tried to explain with the example of two brothers of the same family. Likewise, DJIA and DJTA are the two indices of the

U.S., and as per Dow Theory- Both indices should move in the same direction, which shows the strength in the primary trend. If both move inversely, that indicates the strength of the trend is weak.

The logic is simple behind this theory; Dow believed that if the business performed better, so the transportation would also perform well. If the business is performing and transport companies are not performing, then it is a sign of reversal or weak strength of the trend and vice-versa. That's why Dow theory states both indices should confirm each other moves.

1. **Volume should confirm the trend:** It's a simple concept again. Let's assume you are living in a different city for your studies. Your parent spends a lot on your studies. You are getting the funds as per your wants. And this pattern kept on rising. As you grow and get class promotions, your expense will also rise. So, the twist is what makes this pattern, or you may say the rising expense trend continues? It's your result. Your good result can support all your drama and expenses in front of your parents if you keep on increasing your living expense and not showing the result. The trend of money flow from your parents may stop anytime.

Likewise: If the market moves in a trend there should have sufficient volume to support the trend. The trend of the market and Volume should be in the same direction.

Don't worry; you will get to know about the volume in the upcoming chapter.

Trend continuous until a reversal occurs : Bina break lagaaye gaari nhi rukti. This is the explanation of this point. Yes, you read it right. As per Dow theory, the trend continuous until some outer factors involve force the price to fall, which leads to a change the trend. The outer factors convey the market participants to buy or sell to change the trend of the market.

We are talking about price actions from the 1st chapter and analysis of price. We can't do analysis in mind. We need to plot the data. And connect the dots to identify the pattern.

Here comes the concept of a chart.

What is Chart?

It is nothing but just a graph. But a very crucial part of Technical Analysis. You just need to plot the data or price in case of trading. To plot the chart, you need to plot the Price on Y-Axis(Vertically) and time on X-Axis(Horizontally). This graph will show you the movement of price over a specific time period. This plotting forms a diagram through which technical analysts analyze the trend in the market. And tries to find the opportunity to trade. See the chart in the figure below.

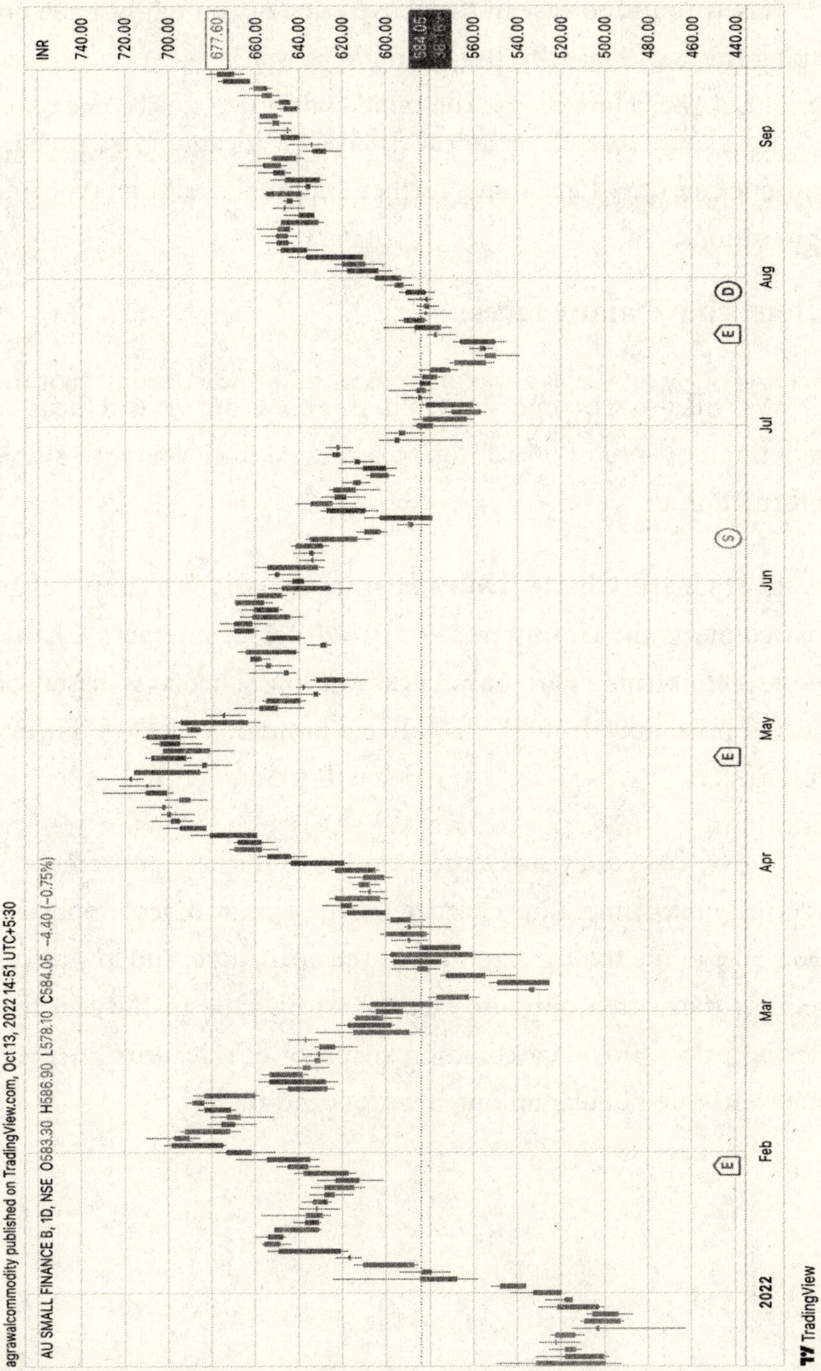
agrawalcommodity published on TradingView.com, Oct 13, 2022 14:51 UTC+5:30
AU SMALL FINANCE B, 1D, NSE O583.30 H586.90 L578.10 C584.05 −4.40 (−0.75%)
INR
740.00
720.00
700.00
677.60
660.00
640.00
620.00
600.00
584.05
560.00
540.00
520.00
500.00
480.00
460.00
440.00
2022
Feb
Mar
Apr
May
Jun
Jul
Aug
Sep
TradingView

It may sound so easy in the above lines, or you might feel I am taking this topic casually. But it's not true.

This is the core of Technical Analysis. We cannot imagine TA without charting. Let's move further and understand its type and applications.

Charts have many faces:

We will also see some of them in this book, but we will focus on only the most useful one; I don't want to confuse you with ample information.

Line Chart (Charles Dow's favorite chart): It's a simple chart that connects the closing price of two different intervals. Charles Dow prefers this chart only because Dow Theory is based on closing price only. It might look like a limitation of Dow Theory. Yes, it is.

It gives traders a visual representation of the price movement of a security over time. Line charts remove noise from less important moments in the trading day, such as the open, high, and low prices, because they often only use closing prices. Due to the fact that closing prices provide a common snapshot of a security's activity, line charts are popular among investors and traders.

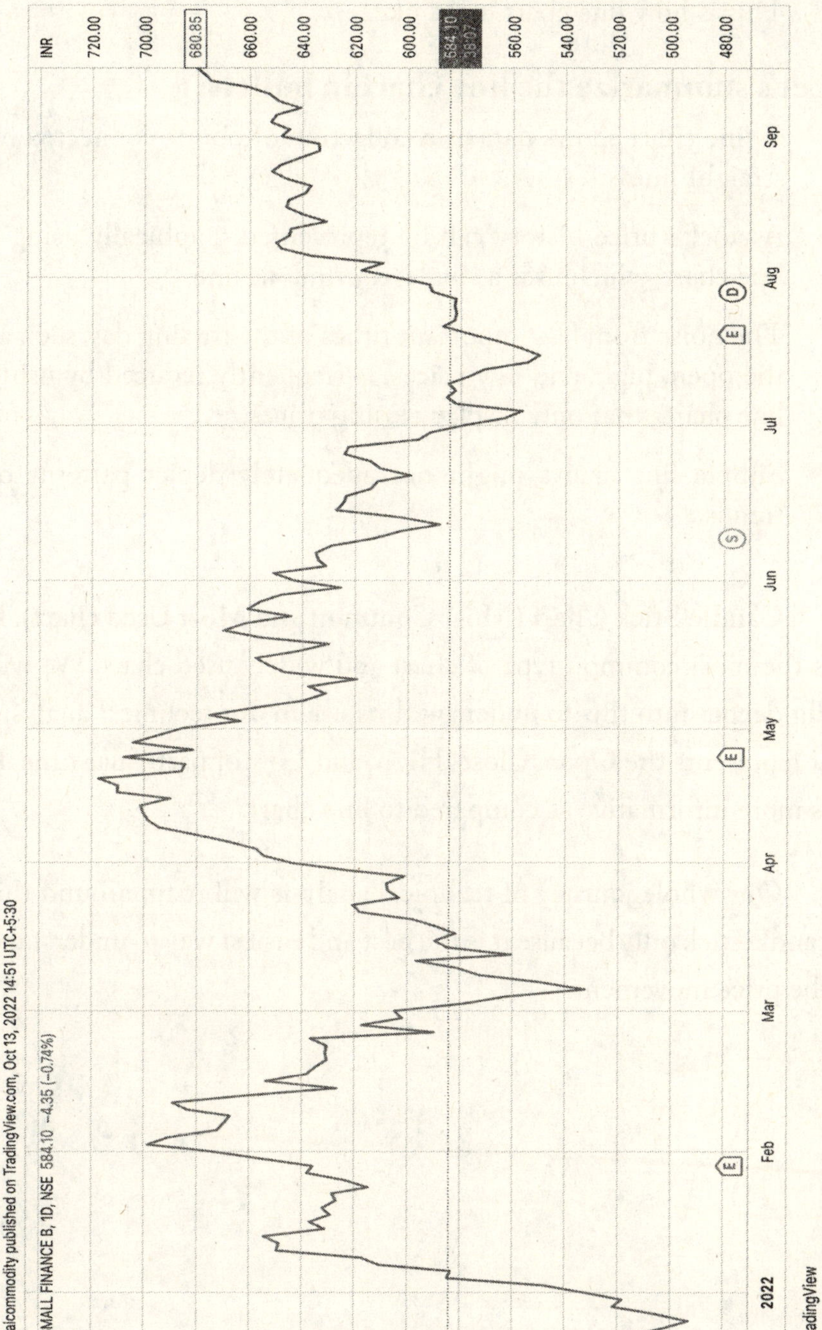
agrawalcommodity published on TradingView.com, Oct 13, 2022 14:51 UTC+5:30
AU SMALL FINANCE B, 1D, NSE 584.10 −4.35 (−0.74%)
INR
720.00
700.00
680.85
660.00
640.00
620.00
600.00
584.10
560.00
540.00
520.00
500.00
480.00
2022
Feb
Mar
Apr
May
Jun
Jul
Aug
Sep
TradingView

This is how line chart looks like.

Let's summarize the line chart in bullets:

- A line chart shows data as a collection of points connected by straight lines.
- A stock's price history can be represented graphically using a line chart, which uses a single, continuous line.
- The noise from less important times of the trading day, such as the open, high, and low prices, is frequently reduced by using line charts that only display closing prices.
- Simple line charts might not adequately depict patterns or trends.

Candle Stick Chart (Most Common and Most Used chart): It is the most common type of chart and widely used chart. We will dig deeper into this to understand its use in our technical analysis. It represents the Open, Close, High, and Low of particular time. It is more informative as compared to line chart.

Our whole journey of technical analysis will roam around this candle stick only because it is the best and easiest way to understand the price movement.

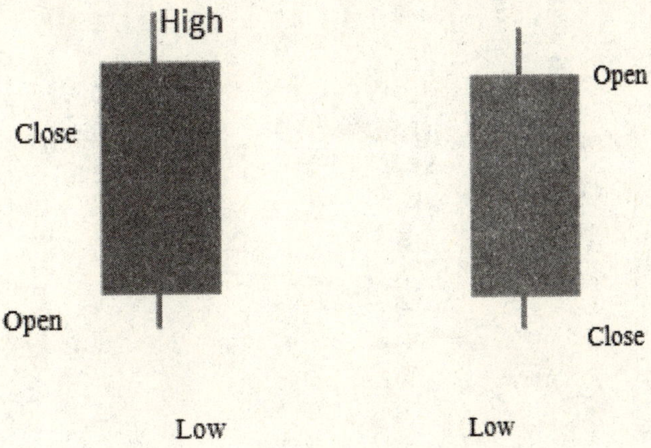

As you can see in the candles above, the green one represents bullish momentum in which the Close is higher than the Open.

The red candle represents the bearish momentum in which Close is lower than Open.

It conveys that emotion by visually illustrating the magnitude of price movements with various hues.

To predict the short-term direction of the price, traders utilize candlesticks to make trading decisions based on recurring patterns.

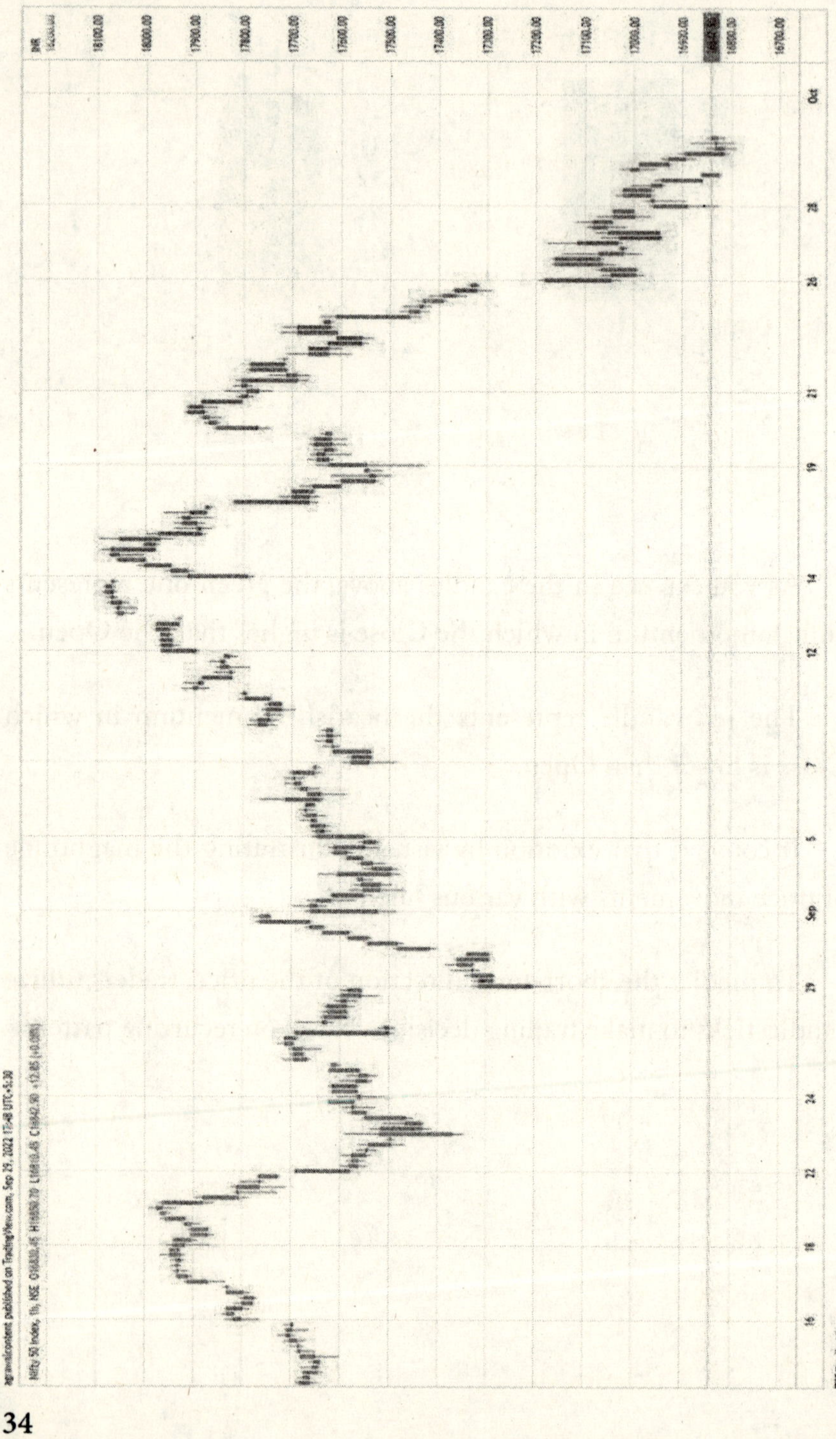

Let's summarize the candlestick chart in bullets:

- Traders use candlestick charts to predict potential price movement based on historical trends.

- When trading, candlesticks are helpful since they display four price points (open, close, high, and low) over the specified time period.

- The same price data displayed in candlestick charts serve as the foundation for numerous algorithms.

- Trading decisions are frequently influenced by emotions, which are visible in candlestick charts.

In upcoming chapters, you will also learn the candle stick pattern, which really works and give trading opportunities.

HeikinAshi Chart (Big Brother of Candle Stick Chart): I call this candle Big brother of Candle stick. Because it looks like a candle only, but the difference is that it shows the average price. Like: In this candle closing price will be the average of the Open, Close, High, and Low of the previous day, and Open Price will be the Open and Close of the previous day's candle. Because it shows the average price, it is also called an Average bar.

While trading, the Heikin-Ashi approach can be used in conjunction with candlestick charts to identify market trends and forecast future prices. It helps make candlestick charts easier to read and trends simpler to analyze.

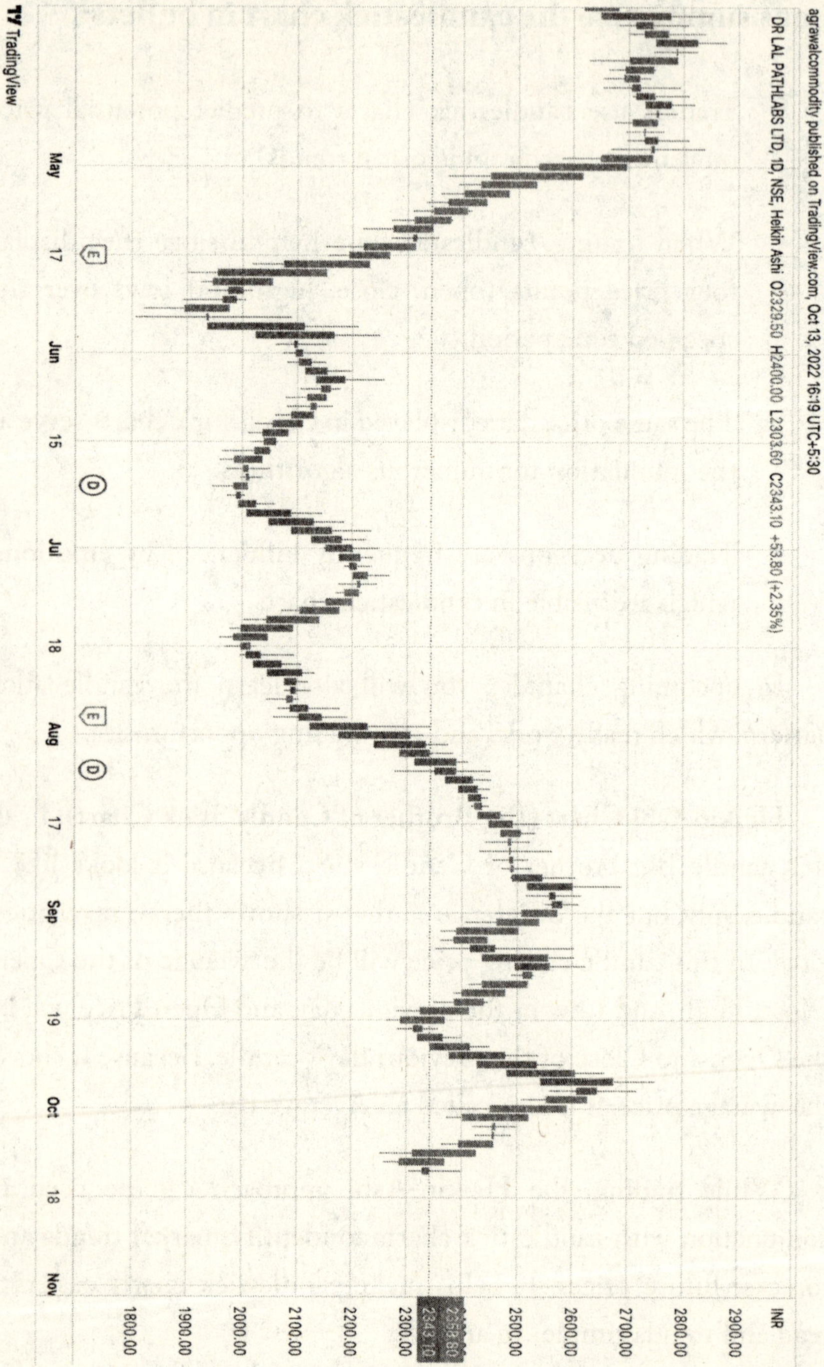
agrawalcommodity published on TradingView.com, Oct 13, 2022 16:19 UTC+5:30
DR LAL PATHLABS LTD, 1D, NSE, Heikin Ashi O2329.50 H2400.00 L2303.60 C2343.10 +53.80 (+2.35%)
INR
2900.00
2800.00
2700.00
2600.00
2500.00
2358.80
2343.10
2300.00
2200.00
2100.00
2000.00
1900.00
1800.00
May
17
Jun
15
Jul
18
Aug
17
Sep
19
Oct
18
Nov
TradingView

This is how Heikin-Ashi Chart looks like.

Let's summarize the Heikin-Ashi Chart pattern:

- Traders can use candlestick charts and the Heikin-Ashi approach to identify and analyze trends.
- Heikin-Ashi charts employ five main indications for their analysis.

1. Strong upward trends are indicated by hollow or green candles without any lower "shadows": Let your earnings soar!
2. Green or hollow candles indicate an upward trend. Perhaps you should increase your long position and reduce your short positions.
3. A change in trend is indicated by candles with a small body surrounded by upper and lower shadows: While some traders will wait for confirmation before going long or short, risk-loving traders may buy or sell here.
4. You might wish to increase your short position and reduce your long position if you see filled or red candles, which suggest a downtrend.
5. Strong downtrends are indicated by filled or red candles with no higher shadows: Till the trend changes, keep it short.

Bar Chart

This is the advanced version of the line chart, you can say. I am saying so because it formed from a line only, but the difference is that in line chart we only plot closing price, but in bar chart, Open, Close, High, Low all the data is plotted.

A bar chart is a group of price bars that display price changes over a specific time period. The high and low prices achieved during the period are shown by a vertical line that runs the length of each bar. A small horizontal line indicates the closing price to the right of the vertical line, and a small horizontal line indicates the opening price to the left.

The bar may be tinted green if the closing price is higher than the open price. On the other hand, if the close is lower than the open, the price fell during that time, so it can be highlighted in red.

Bar charts—or other chart types like candlestick or line charts—are used by technical analysts to track price action, which helps them make trading decisions. Trades can be made using bar charts to assess trends, identify potential trend reversals, and track volatility and price changes.

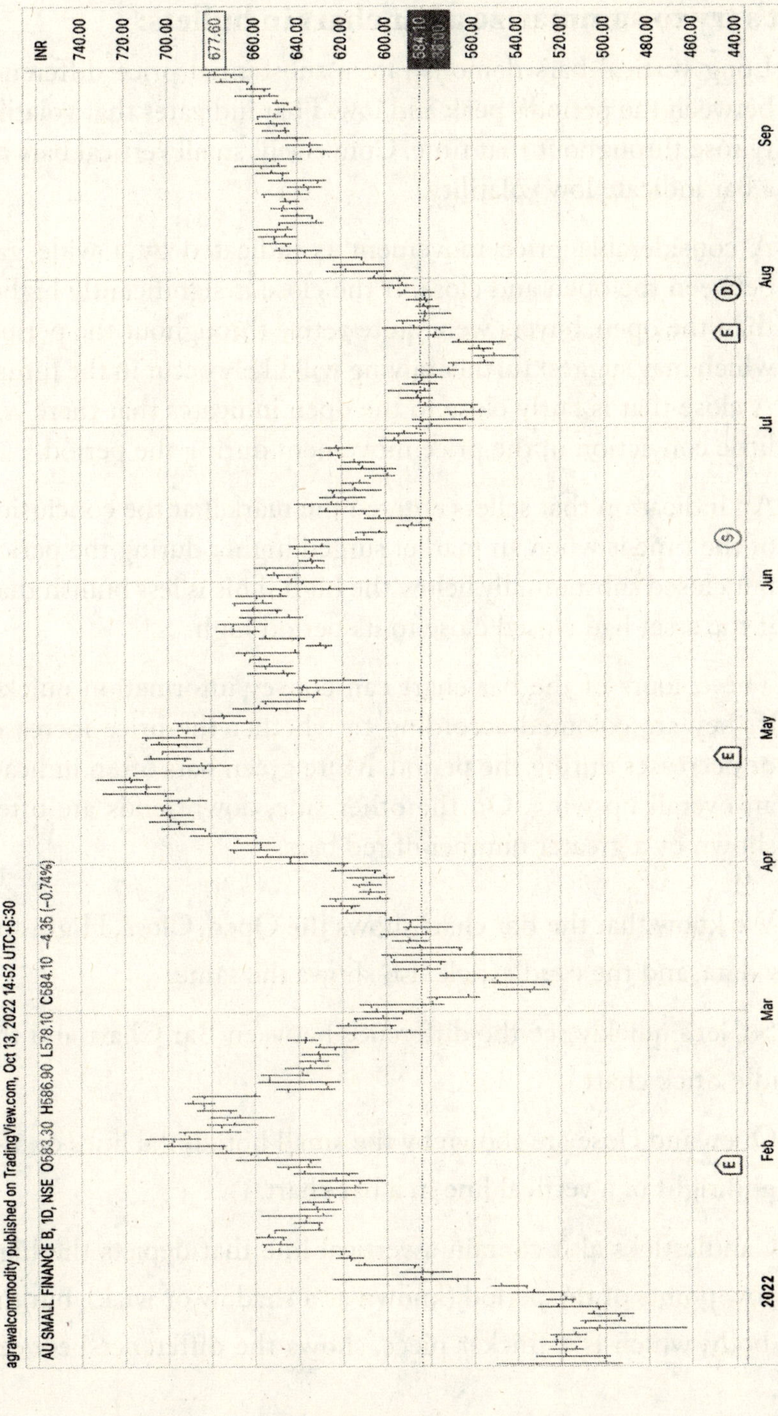
agrawalcommodity published on TradingView.com, Oct 13, 2022 14:52 UTC+5:30
AU SMALL FINANCE B, 1D, NSE O583.30 H586.90 L578.10 C584.10 −4.35 (−0.74%)
INR
740.00
720.00
700.00
677.60
660.00
640.00
620.00
600.00
584.10
560.00
540.00
520.00
500.00
480.00
460.00
440.00
2022
Feb
Mar
Apr
May
Jun
Jul
Aug
Sep
TradingView

Let's try to summarize a bar chart in bullets:

- Long vertical bars demonstrate a substantial price difference between the period's peak and low. That indicates that volatility rose throughout that time. Conversely, small vertical bars on a bar indicate low volatility.

- A considerable price movement is indicated by a wide gap between the open and close. If the close is significantly higher than the open, buyers were quite active throughout the period, which may suggest further buying will likely occur in the future. A close that is fairly close to the open indicates that there was little conviction in the price movement during the period.

- An indication that sellers entered the market at the conclusion of the time is when an market surged higher during the period but closed substantially below the high. This is less bullish than if the asset had closed close to its period high.

- The colours of the bar chart can convey information quickly if they are coloured according to whether the price increases or decreases during the period. More green bars often indicate an overall upswing. On the other side, downtrends are often shown by a greater number of red bars.

We know that the Bar chart shows the Open, Close, High, and Low data, and the candlestick also shows the same.

So, let's quickly see the difference between Bar Chart and the Candle Stick chart.

Open and close are shown by the small horizontal lines on the left and right of a vertical line in a bar chart.

Candlesticks also contain a vertical line that depicts the high and low points of the period (known as a shadow or wick), but the real body, which is a thicker piece, shows the difference between the open and close. The body is shaded or colored red if the close is below the open and white, green, or blue if the close is above the open. Despite the fact that the information in the two types of charts is the same, they seem very different.

Bar Chart

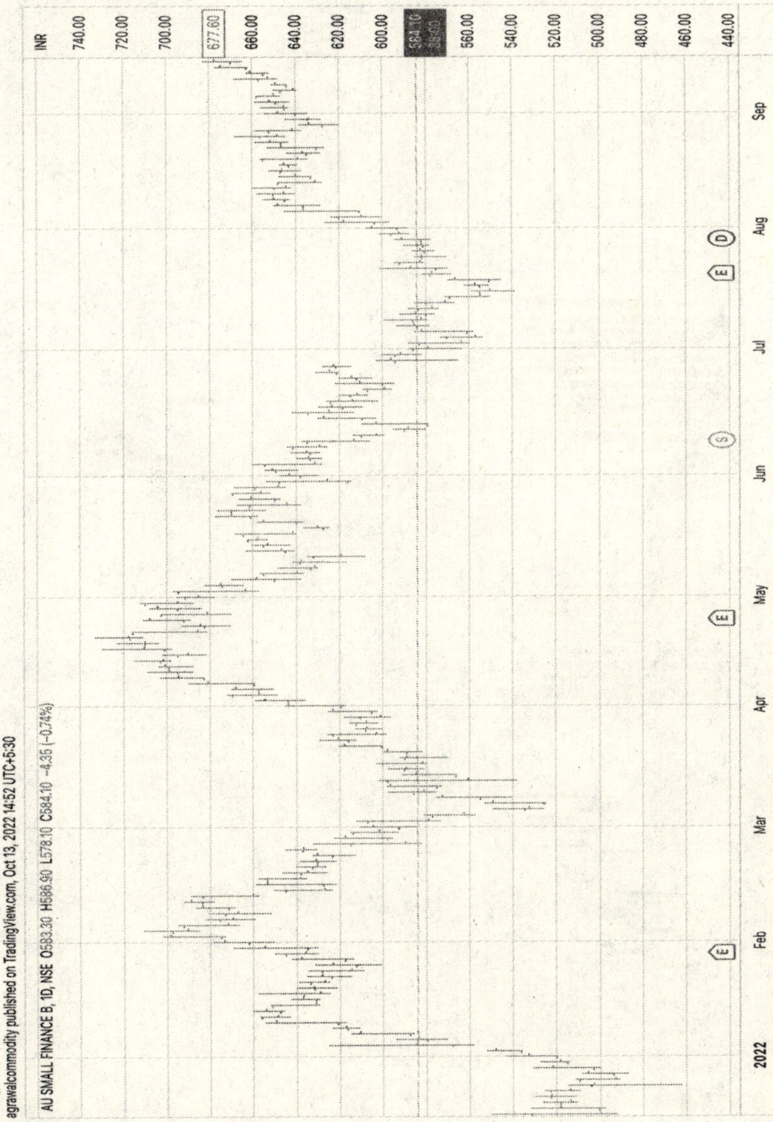

CandleStick Chart :

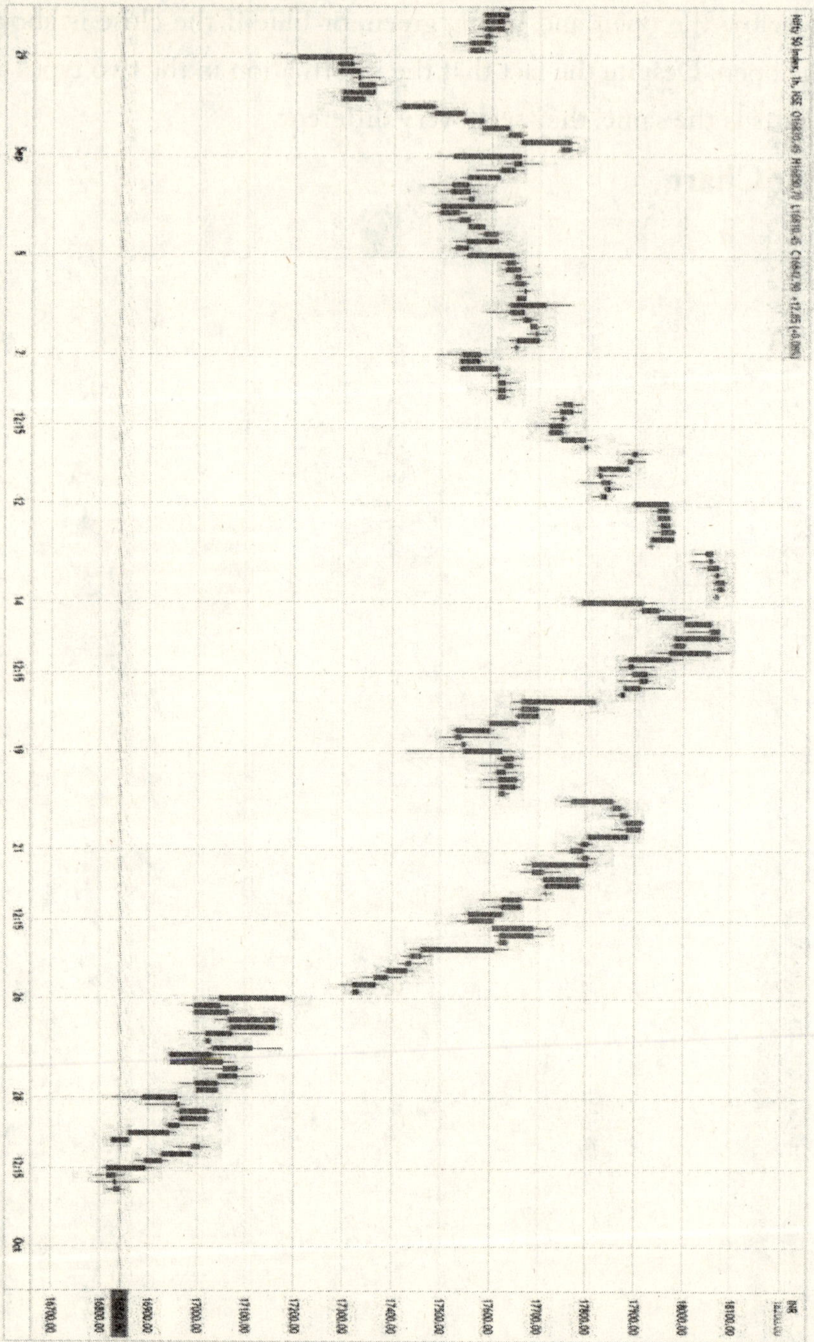

Now we will learn some chart patterns you find most often in the market. That helps in trading.

What is Chart Pattern?

Have you ever observed your friend's behavior and predicted his next move?

Have you ever predicted the next action of your favorite player while watching the match?

Yes, Right?

But why am I talking about these things?

What is the correlation between this human behavior and chart pattern?

Well, as you read your friend's behavior and playing technique of your favorite player, this enables you to predict their future move.

The same concepts work in chart patterns also. Chart patterns are nothing but the behavior of price movement, which forms a shape through which analyst predicts the future move of the price.

Double Bottom :

This is a bullish pattern. To form this pattern price hits the support price twice before moving upside.

It looks like "W" on the chart. Let's assume a stock price starts at Rs. 100; whenever the stock price hits 60, it moves back towards 80, then again it moves back to 60, and then after touching 60, it moves back to 80 or 100. Analysts believe that if the price breaks out above the highest point of the pattern, the price may rise further.

What does it show? It shows that some market participants are sitting at Rs. 60 levels to buy the stocks at that 60, which holds the stock price above 60 and

furthers pushed back to 80 or 100. You, as an analyst, observed this behavior of stock price movement.

But what indicates to you that this is the right time to buy? It is when the stock price moves above its highest price from where it starts falling.

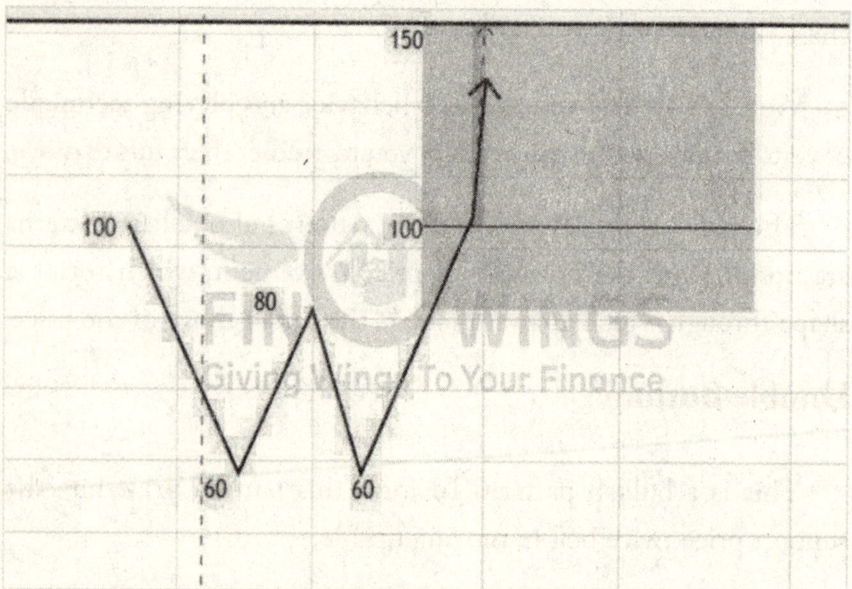

As you can see in the above figure. This is all about the Double Bottom or "W" chart pattern.

Traders can go long above the high of the pattern with the SL of the high of the middle peak.

This is also called a Bullish reversal pattern because it is found during a falling market.

Double Top Pattern

This pattern is just a mirror image of a double bottom. You can find this during the up trend, and this pattern indicates a reversal. It looks like "M" on the chart.

Let's assume a stock price starts at Rs. 100; whenever the stock price hits 150, it moves back towards 125, then again it moves back to 150, and then after touching 150, it moves back to 125 or 100. Analysts believe that if the price breaks below the lowest point of the pattern, then the price may fall further.

What does it show?

It shows that some market participants are sitting at Rs. 150 level to sell the stocks at 150, which holds the stock price below 150 and furthers pushed back to 125 or 100. You, as an analyst, observed this behavior of stock price movement. But what indicates to you that this is the right time to sell? It is when the stock price moves below its lowest price from where it starts rising.

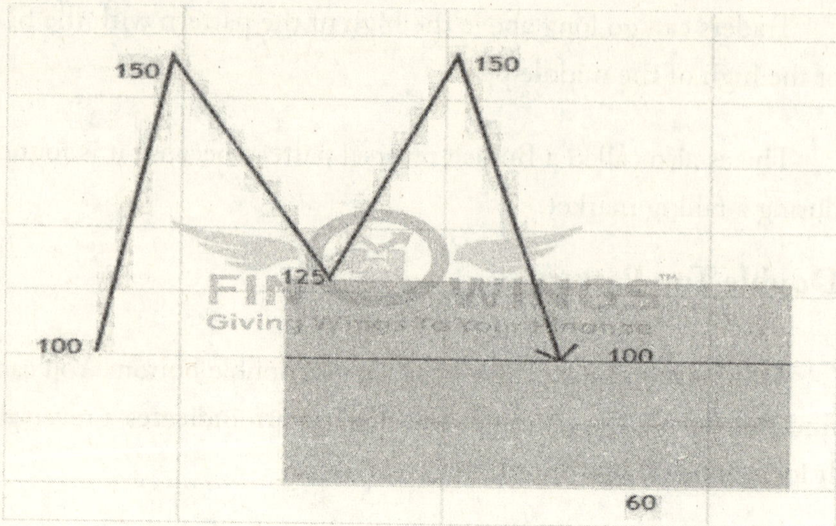

As you can see in the above figure. This is all about the Double Top or "M" chart pattern.

Traders can go short below the Low of the pattern with the SL of the Low of the middle.

This is also called a Bearish reversal pattern because it is found during a rising market.

Head and Shoulder Pattern

This pattern is formed with three peaks, in which the 1st and 3rd peaks are longer than the 2nd peak.

All the peaks stand on a point called a Neckline.

It forms the shape of a head and shoulder at the top, hence indicating the reversal in the market.

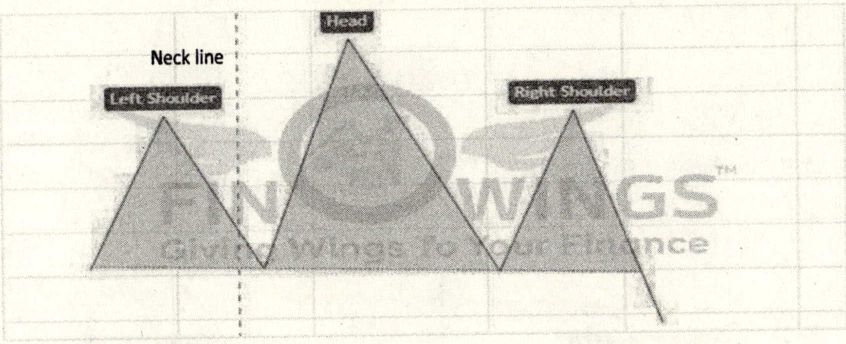

This is what head and shoulder patterns look like. This shows that the price is trying to move up, but market participants are not willing to trade this share above the specific price, which forms the peak of the pattern. This pattern leads the price

towards low, and analysts believe that if the price breaks below the neckline, it may fall further.

Traders can create a short position below the neckline with the SL of the neckline

Inverse head and shoulder

This pattern works exactly in reverse of the head and shoulder pattern. You can find this pattern at the bottom, which further leads to the bullish reversal.

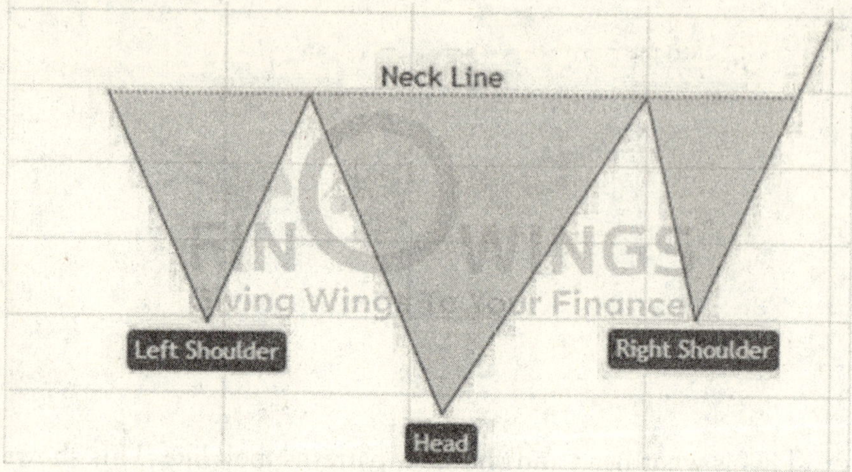

This is what an inverse head and shoulder pattern looks like. This shows that the price is trying to move down, but market participants are bullish and want to buy at every dip. This pattern leads the price above the high of the neckline; an analyst believes that if the price breaks above the neckline, it may rise further.

A trader can create a long position above the neckline with the SL of the Neckline.

Flag Pattern

You can find this pattern anywhere in between any trend. This is a continuous pattern that forms after a significant rally.

Let's assume a bullish flag pattern in our example.

The market gave a rally from 1000 to 1500; after that, it started trading in a parallel range more similar to the distribution phase. This behavior of price forms a bullish flag pattern.

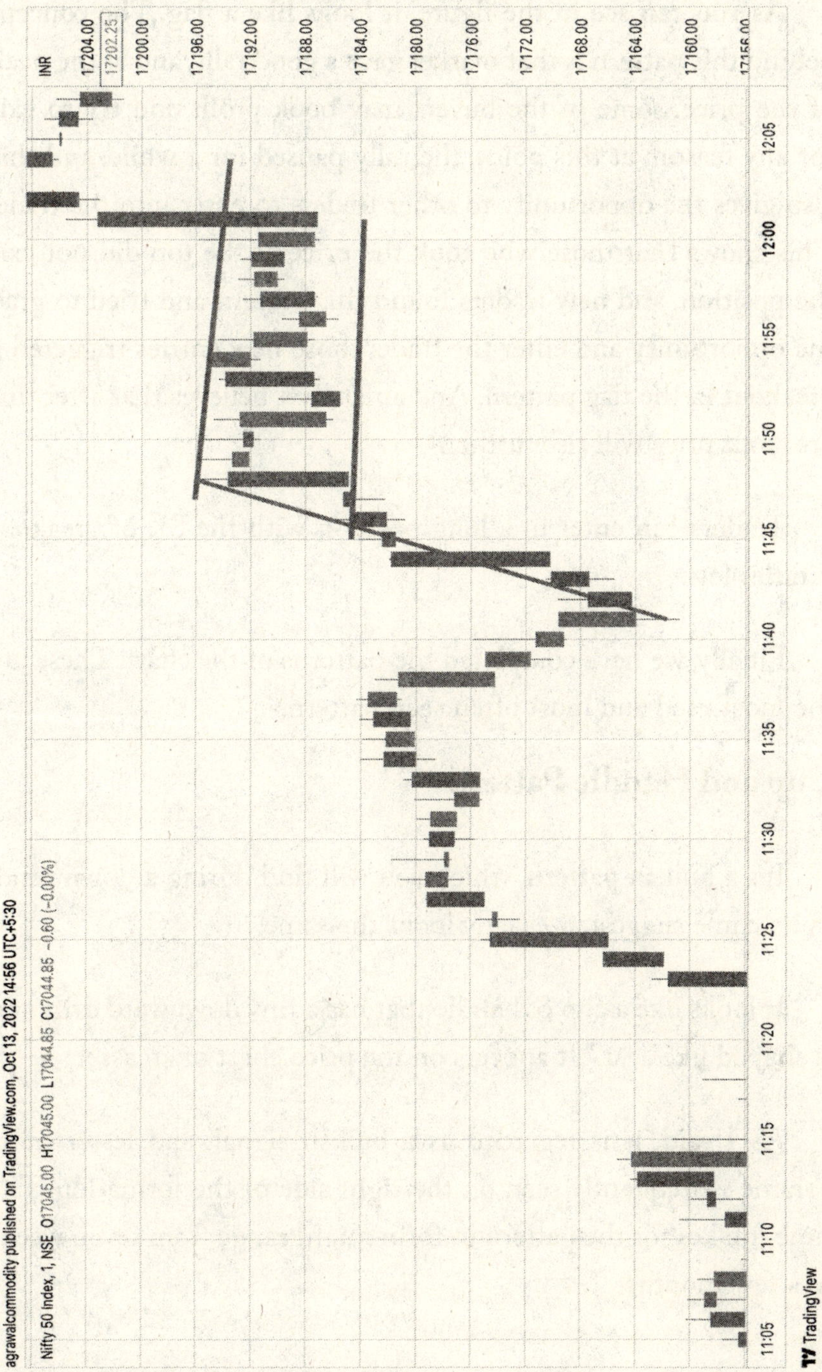
agrawalcommodity published on TradingView.com, Oct 13, 2022 14:56 UTC+5:30
Nifty 50 Index, 1, NSE O17045.00 H17045.00 L17044.85 C17044.85 −0.60 (−0.00%)
INR
17204.00
17202.25
17200.00
17196.00
17192.00
17188.00
17184.00
17180.00
17176.00
17172.00
17168.00
17164.00
17160.00
17156.00
12:05
12:00
11:55
11:50
11:45
11:40
11:35
11:30
11:25
11:20
11:15
11:10
11:05
TradingView

As you can see in the figure, it looks like a flag. The concept behind this pattern is that market gave a good rally, and at the peak of the price, some of the buyers may book profit and try to exit for any reason; at this point, the rally paused for a while, and this also gives the opportunity to other traders to enter into the trade. This shows that those who took the price at the top did not exit the position, and new traders found this pattern and tried to grab the opportunity and enter the trade; those new entries triggered a breakout in the flag pattern. And an analyst believes that after this breakout price will rise further.

Traders can enter in a long position with the SL of breakout candles low.

Finally, we have completed the patterns of the chart. These are the most used and most often seen pattern.

Cup and Handle Pattern

It's a bullish pattern, which you will find during a downtrend; as its name suggest, it exactly looks the same.

It looks like a cup & handle that has a tiny downward drift and is shaped like a "u." It appears on the price chart of an asset.

As I said, it is regarded as a bullish signal, and lesser trade volume is frequently seen on the right side of the formation. The time it takes for the pattern to form might range from seven weeks to a few months.

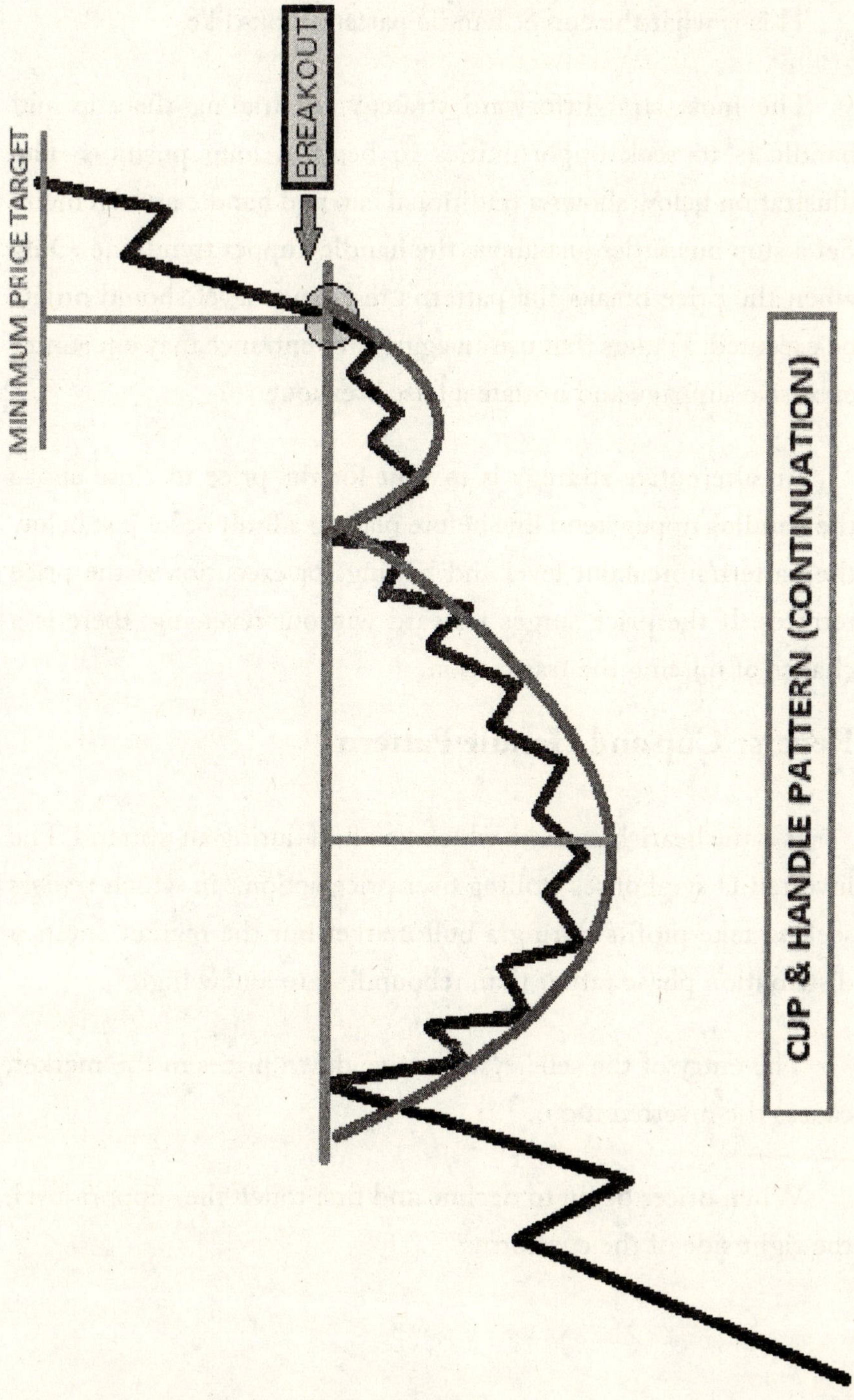
MINIMUM PRICE TARGET
BREAKOUT
CUP & HANDLE PATTERN (CONTINUATION)

This is what the cup & handle pattern looks like.

The most straightforward strategy for trading the cup and handle is to seek opportunities to begin a long position. The illustration below shows a traditional cup and handle arrangement. Set a stop buy order just above the handle's upper trend line. Only when the price breaks the pattern's resistance level should orders be executed. Traders that use an aggressive entrance may encounter excessive slippage and initiate a false breakout.

An alternative strategy is to wait for the price to close above the handle's upper trend line before placing a limit order just below the pattern's breakout level and hoping for execution if the price retraces. If the price surges forward without reversing, there is a chance of missing the transaction.

Reverse Cup and Handle Pattern

It is the bearish pattern, which you find during an uptrend. The inverted U symbolises "rolling over price action," in which traders seek to take profits during a bull market but the market enters a distribution phase rather than rebounding to a new high.

The entry of the sellers, who drive down prices in the market, causes the inverted top.

When prices begin to decline and first touch the support level, the right side of the cup forms.

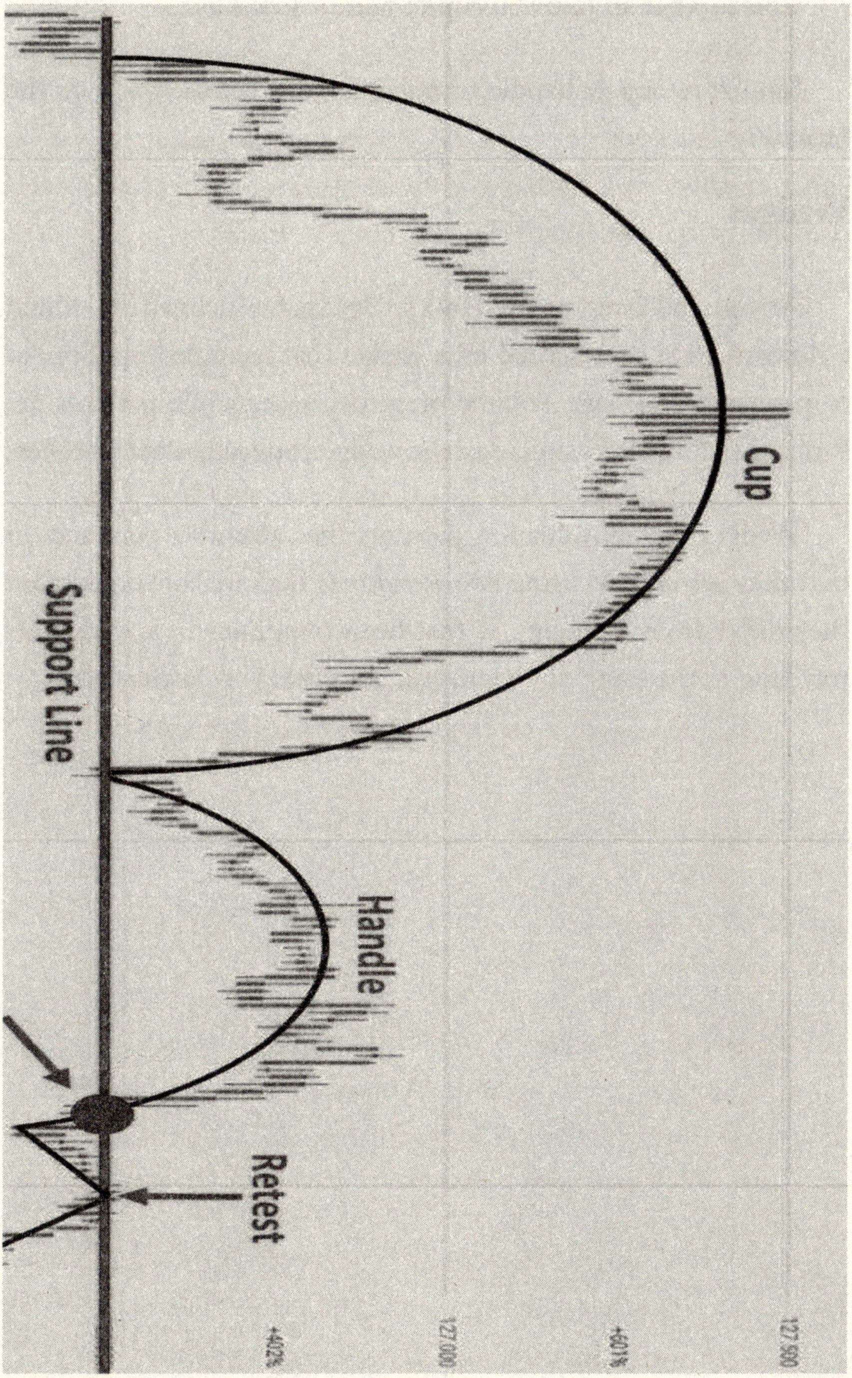
Cup
Support Line
Handle
Retest

This is what an inverted cup & handle looks like.

Similar to cup & handle, a trader can execute the trade on the breakout.

Wedges

An uptrend is represented by a wedge that is inclined down, and a downtrend is represented by a wedge that is angled up. Similar to pennants and flags, volume often decreases while patterns are forming before increasing once the wedge pattern has been broken.

Wedges are continuation patterns that resemble pennants in that they are created using two trendlines that are convergent, but they differ from pennants in that both trendlines in a wedge are traveling in the same direction, either upwards or downward.

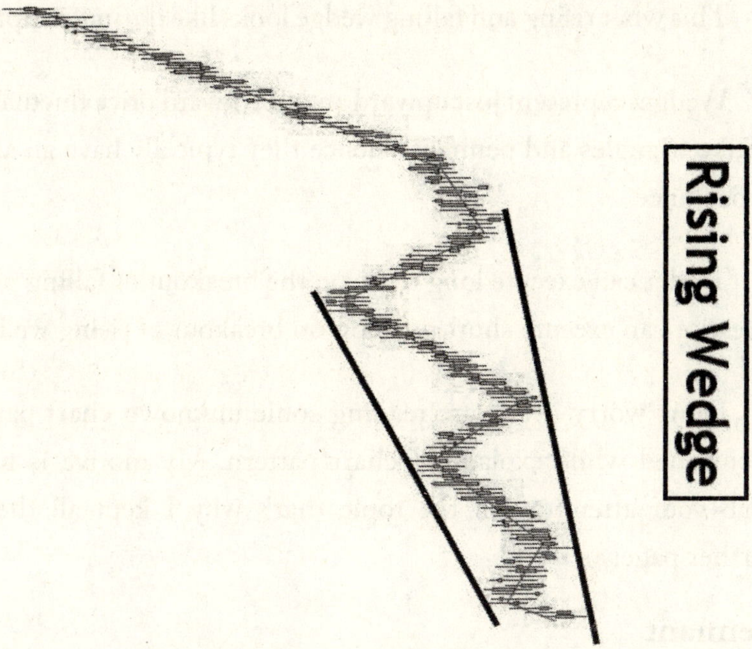
Rising Wedge

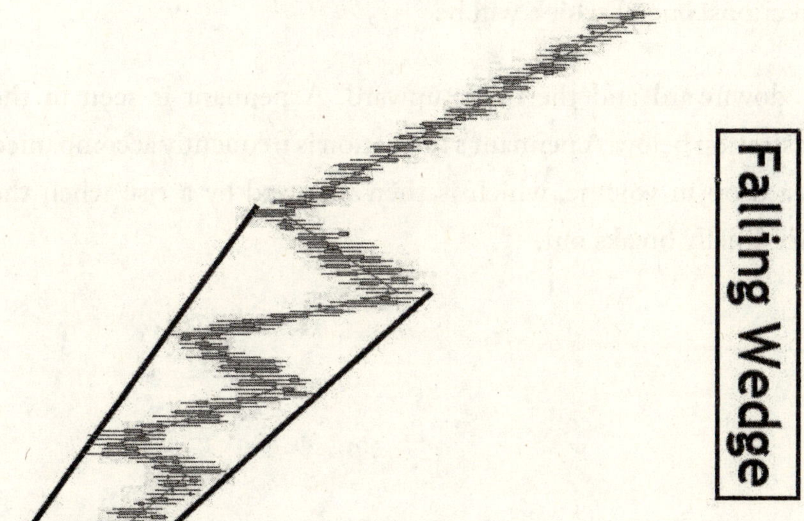
Falling Wedge

This what rising and falling wedge looks like during an uptrend.

Wedges represent just upward and downward price fluctuations, unlike triangles and pennants, hence they typically have an angled appearance.

Trader can execute long trade on the breakout of falling wedge, likewise can execute short position on breakout of rising wedge.

Don't worry if you are reading some unknown chart patterns mentioned while explaining chart pattern. My motive is to just grab your attention on the topic that's why I kept all these in further pages.

Pennant

Pennants are two trendlines that finally converge continuation patterns. Pennants have two trendlines that travel in opposite directions, one of which will be

downward and the other upward. A pennant is seen in the illustration below. A pennant's formation is frequently accompanied by a drop in volume, which is then followed by a rise when the price finally breaks out.

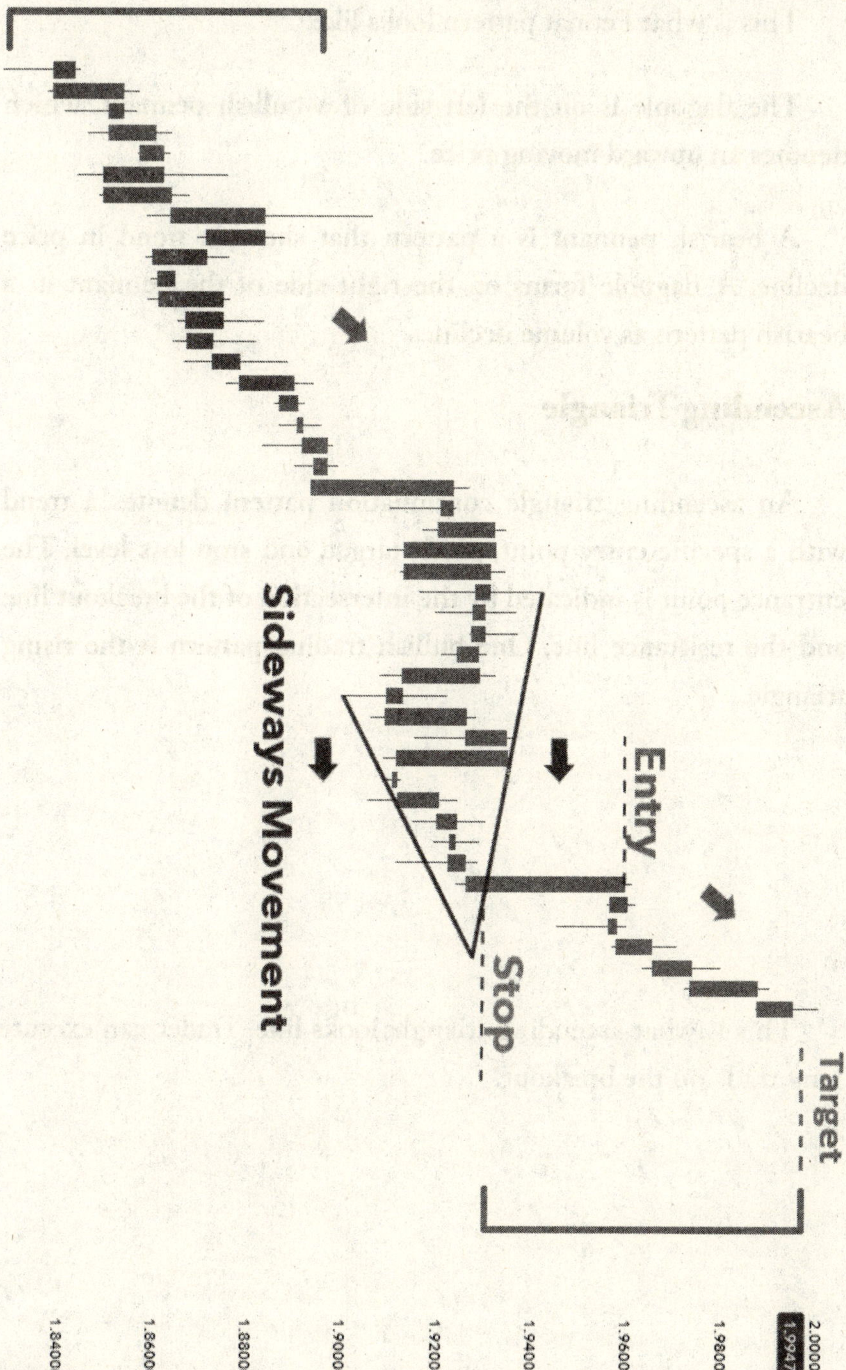
Sideways Movement
Entry
Stop
Target
1.84000
1.86000
1.88000
1.90000
1.92000
1.94000
1.96000
1.98000
1.99474
2.00000

This is what Pennat pattern looks like.

The flagpole is on the left side of a bullish pennant, which denotes an upward moving price.

A bearish pennant is a pattern that shows a trend in price decline. A flagpole forms on the right side of the pennant in a bearish pattern as volume declines.

Ascending Triangle

An ascending triangle continuation pattern denotes a trend with a specific entry point, profit target, and stop loss level. The entrance point is indicated by the intersection of the breakout line and the resistance line. One bullish trading pattern is the rising triangle.

This is what ascending triangle looks like. Trader can execute long trade on the breakout.

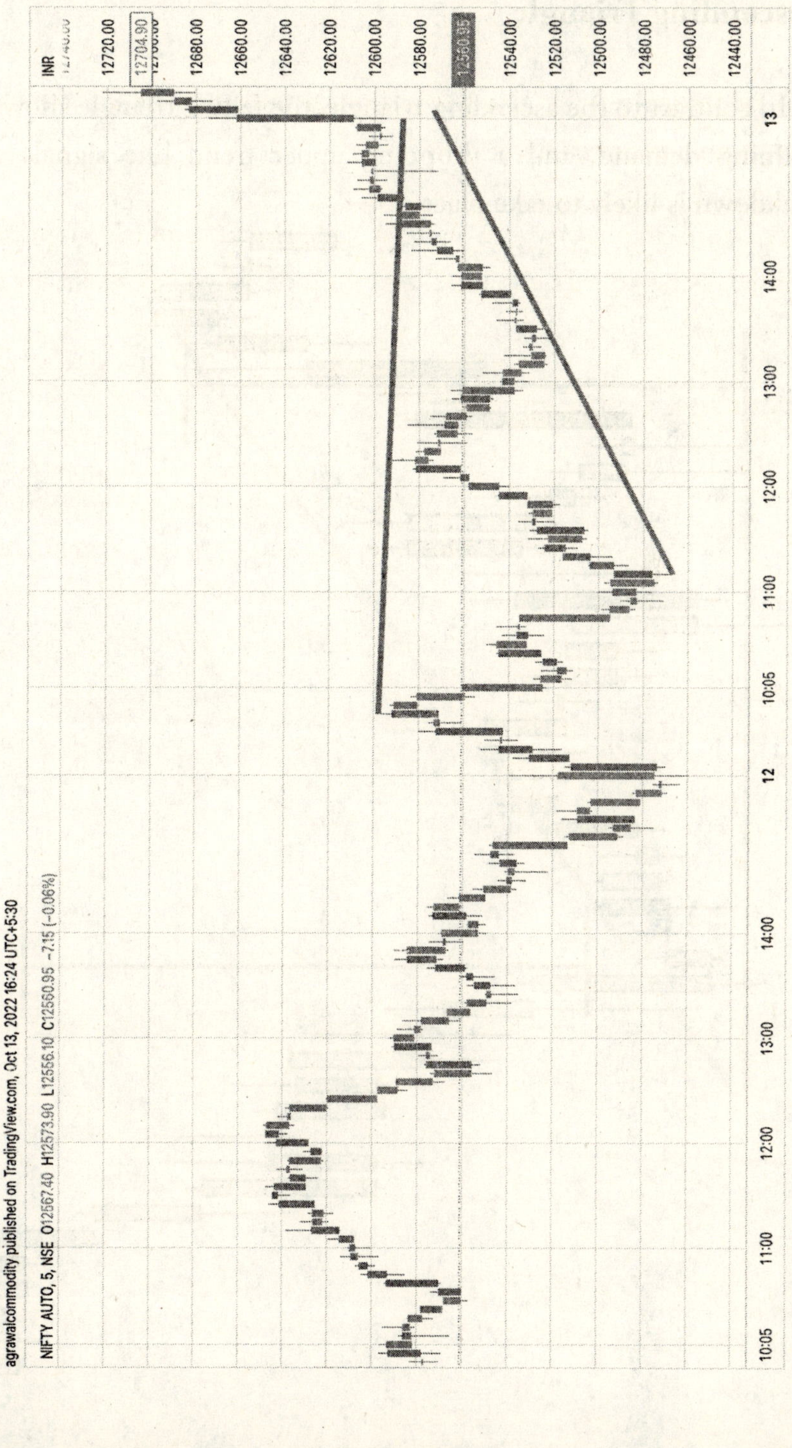
agrawalcommodity published on TradingView.com, Oct 13, 2022 16:24 UTC+5:30
NIFTY AUTO, 5, NSE O12567.40 H12573.90 L12556.10 C12560.95 -7.15 (-0.06%)
INR
12720.00
12704.90
12680.00
12660.00
12640.00
12620.00
12600.00
12580.00
12560.95
12540.00
12520.00
12500.00
12480.00
12460.00
12440.00
10:05
11:00
12:00
13:00
14:00
12
10:05
11:00
12:00
13:00
14:00
13
TradingView

Descending Triangle

In contrast to the ascending triangle, the falling triangle shows declining demand, and a dropping upper trend line signals a breakdown is likely to take place.

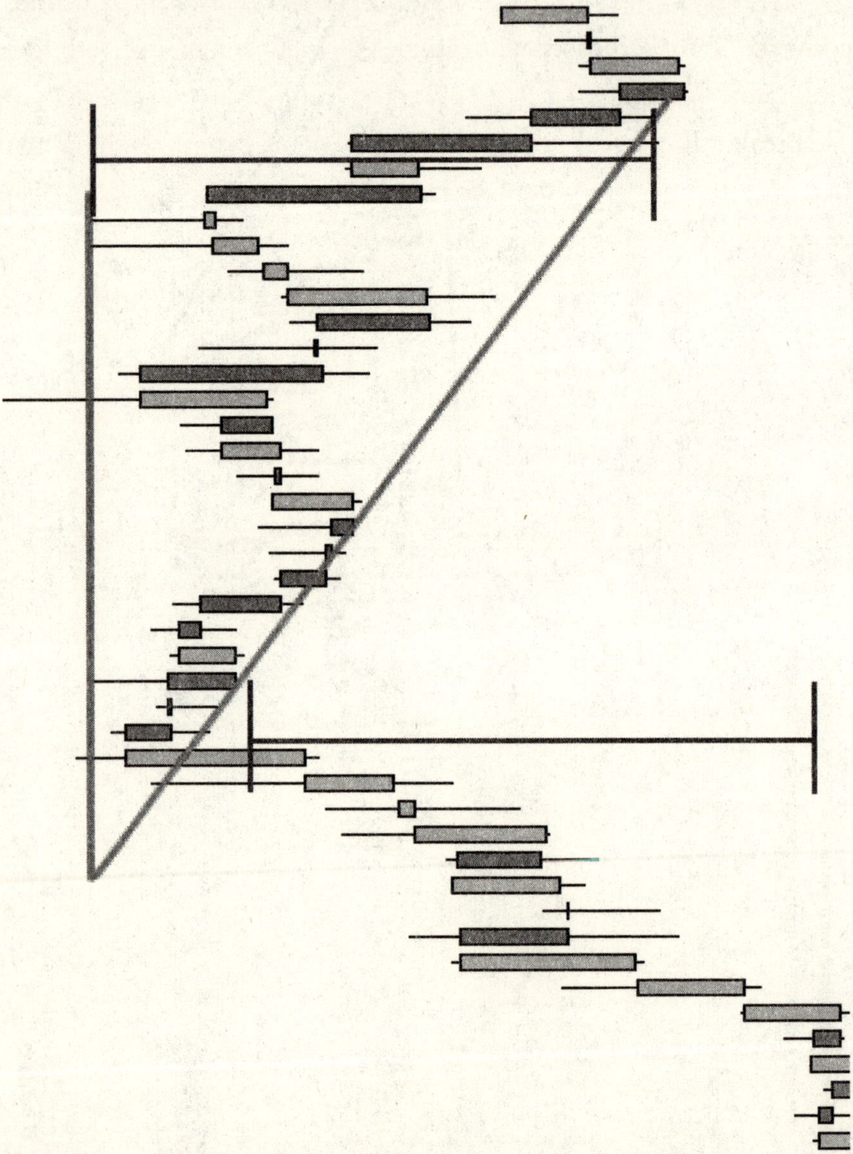

This is what descending triangle pattern looks like. Breakout in either side can trigger the trade.

Symmetrical Triangles

There is no upward or downward trend when two trend lines converge into symmetrical triangles, which solely indicate the likelihood of a breakout. If you see the example below, the size of the breakouts or breakdowns is normally equal to the height of the triangle's left vertical side. Like all other pattern, this pattern also work well on breakouts in either direction.

This is what symmetrical triangle looks like on chart.

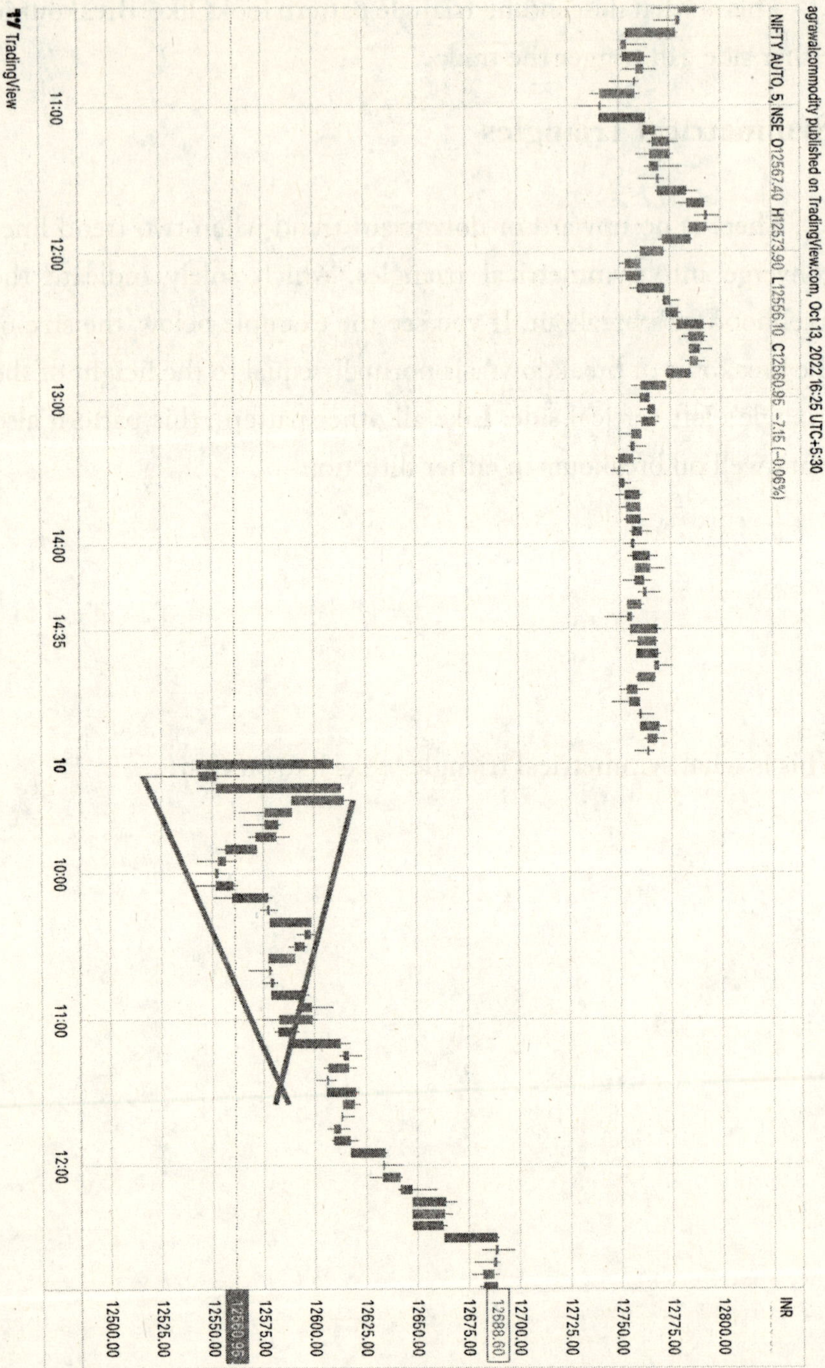
agrawalcommodity published on TradingView.com, Oct 13, 2022 16:25 UTC+5:30
NIFTY AUTO, 5, NSE O12567.40 H12573.90 L12556.10 C12560.95 −7.15 (−0.06%)
TradingView

GAPS

Gaps, or empty spaces on price charts, indicate instances when no shares were traded inside a specific price range.

This typically happens between the market's close on one day and its opening the following day.

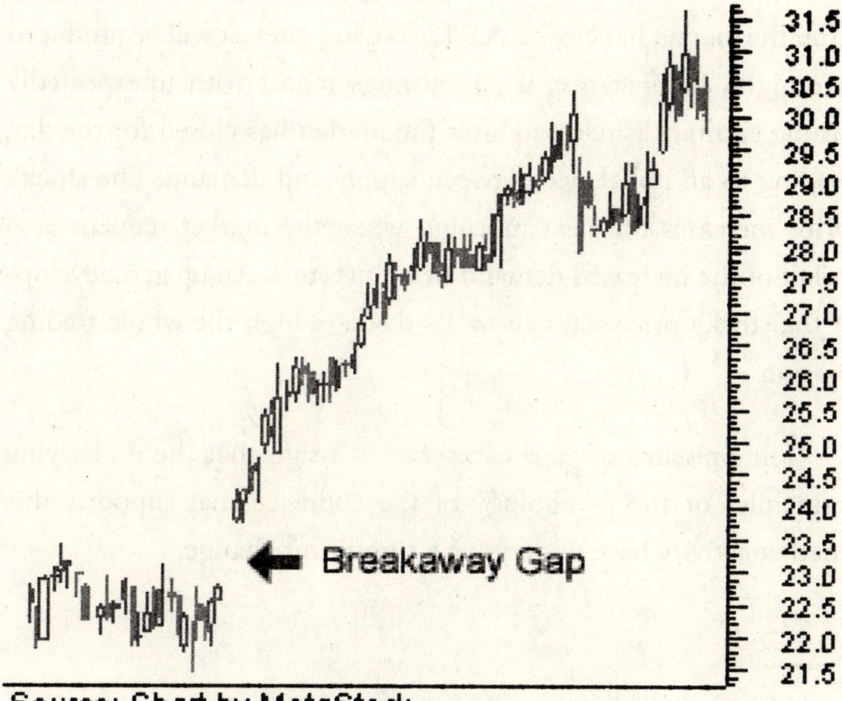

Source: Chart by MetaStock

This is what gap looks like on chart.

Up gaps and down gaps are the two main categories of gaps.

For an upward gap to occur, the market close low price must be greater than the high price of the day. Up gaps are sometimes regarded as bullish. An up gap is the exact opposite of a down gap in that the high price following the market's close must be higher than the low price from the previous day. Down gaps are commonly thought of as bad.

Gaps are caused by unusual buying or selling interest emerging after the market has closed. A lot of buying interest will be produced overnight, for instance, if an earnings report with unexpectedly strong earnings is released after the market has closed for the day, leading to an imbalance between supply and demand. The stock's price increases the next morning when the market reopens as a result of the increased demand from investors. An up gap develops if the stock's price stays above its day-ago high the whole trading session.

The presence of gaps can serve as a sign that the underlying principles or the psychology of the audience that supports this market activity have undergone a significant change.

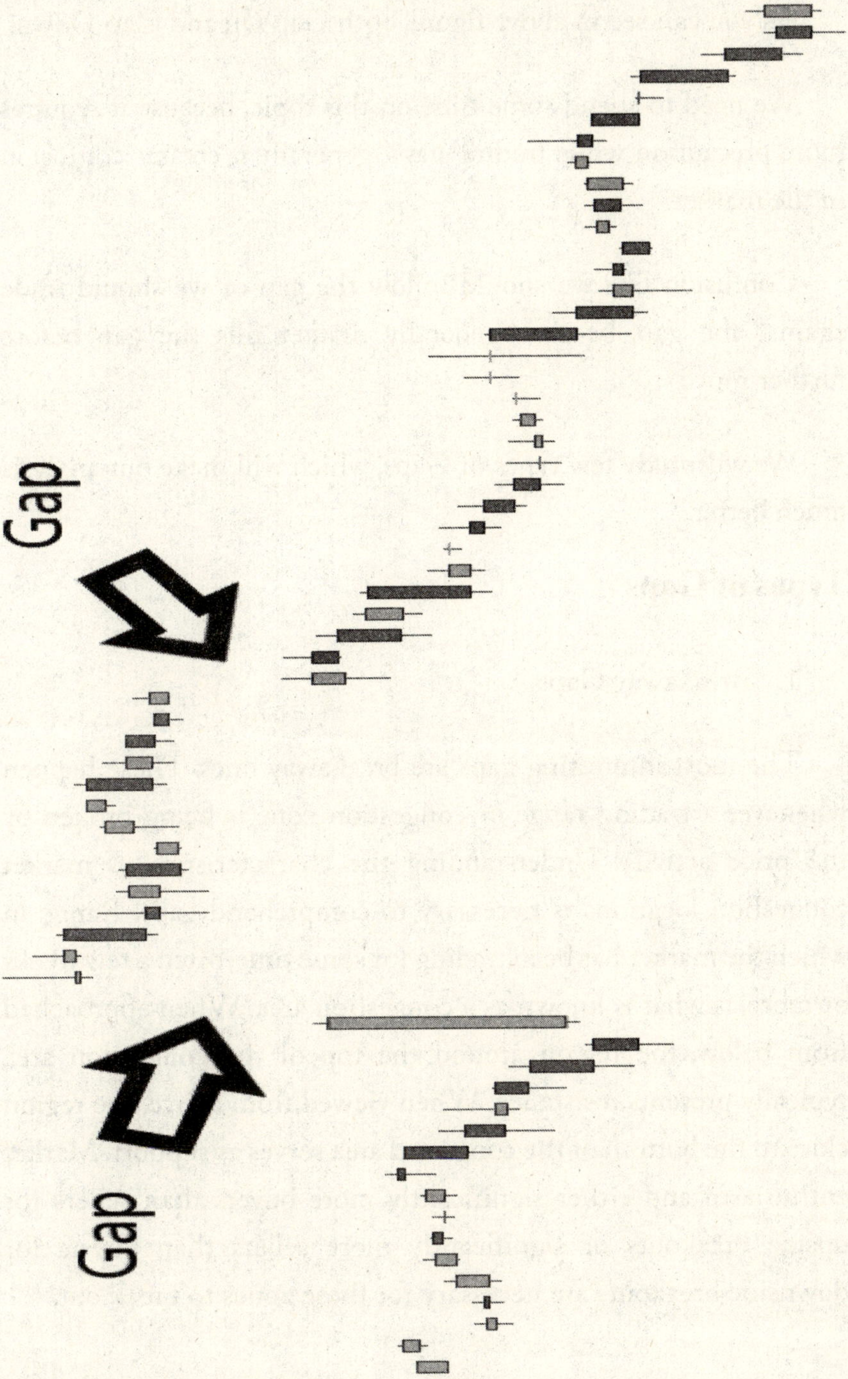
Gap
Gap

As you can see in above figure, both Gap Up and Gap Down.

We need to spend some time on this topic, because it requires more precaution while trading gaps, generally it creates confusion in the market.

Confusion like we should follow the gap or we should trade against the gap, because generally market fills the gap before further move.

We will study few types of Gaps, which will make our analysis much better.

Types of Gaps

1. Breakaway Gaps

The most interesting gaps are breakaway ones. These happen whenever a trading range or congestion zone is being broken by the price activity. Understanding the characteristics of market congestion locations is necessary to comprehend gaps. Range in which the market has been trading for some time, often a few weeks or more, is what is known as a congestion area. When approached from below, the region around the top of the congestion area typically presents resistancc. When viewed from above, the region close to the bottom of the congested area serves as support. Market enthusiasm and either significantly more buyers than sellers for upside breakouts or significantly more sellers than buyers for downside breakouts are necessary for these zones to break out.

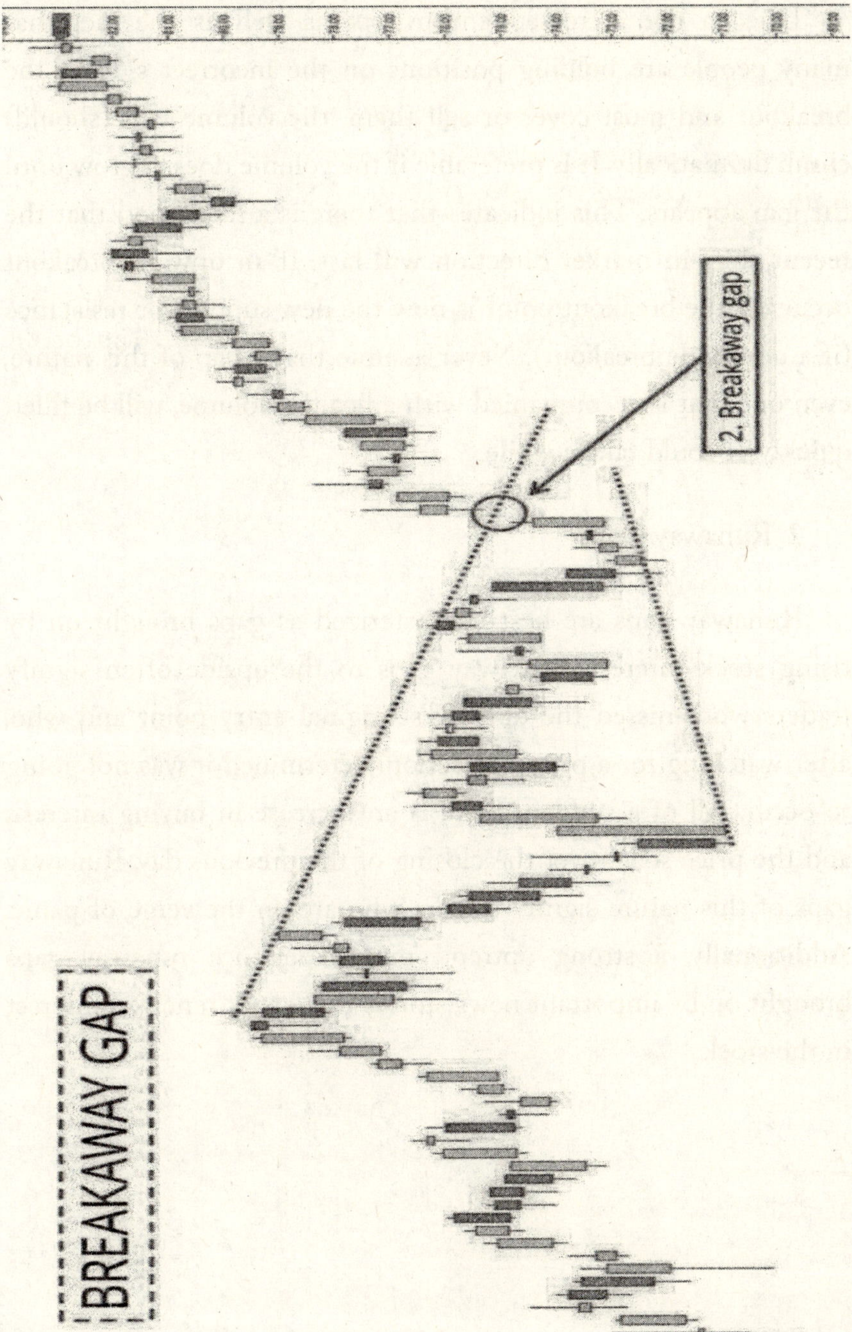
2. Breakaway gap
BREAKAWAY GAP

Due to the increased enthusiasm as well as the fact that many people are holding positions on the incorrect side of the breakout and must cover or sell them, the volume will (should) climb dramatically. It is preferable if the volume doesn't grow until the gap appears. This indicates that there is a likelihood that the recent shift in market direction will last. If an upward breakout occurred, the breakout point is now the new support or resistance (if a downside breakout). Never assume that a gap of this nature, even one that is accompanied with a healthy volume, will be filled quickly. It could take a while.

2. Runaway Gaps

Runaway gaps are best characterized as gaps brought on by rising stock interest. Runaway gaps to the upside often signify traders who missed the uptrend's original entry point and who, after watching for a price correction, determined it was not going to occur. All of a sudden, there is an increase in buying interest, and the price soars over the closing of the previous day. Runaway gaps of this nature signify traders who are on the verge of panic. Additionally, a strong uptrend may experience runaway gaps brought on by important news stories that spark renewed interest in the stock.

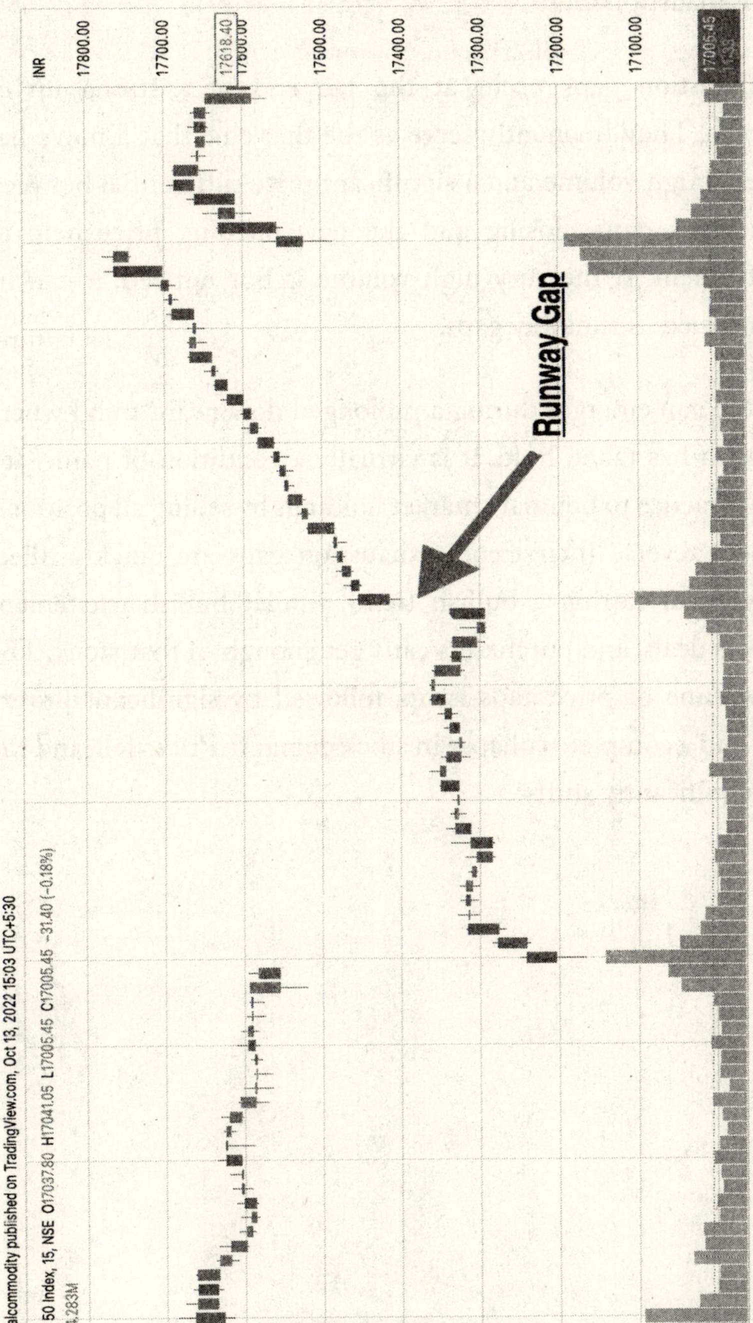
agrawalcommodity published on TradingView.com, Oct 13, 2022 15:03 UTC+5:30
Nifty 50 Index, 15, NSE O17037.80 H17041.05 L17005.45 C17005.45 −31.40 (−0.18%)
Vol 4.283M
Runway Gap
INR
17800.00
17700.00
17618.40
17600.00
17500.00
17400.00
17300.00
17200.00
17100.00
17005.45
26
12:00
14:00
29
12:00
14:00
30
12:00
14:00
Sep
12
TradingView

3. Exhaustion Gaps

Exhaustion gaps occur at the tail end of a strong up or downturn. They frequently serve as the first clue that a move has finished. High volume and a significant price differential between the previous day's closing and the new opening price help to identify them. If the very high volume is not noticed, it can be misconstrued as runaway gaps.

If the gap emerges during a prolonged downward trend where pessimism has taken hold, it is virtually a condition of panic. It's normal practice to liquidate market holdings by selling all positions. As prices reverse their trend, exhaustion gaps are quickly filled. If they occur during a bullish trend, similar bullish excitement overtakes deals, and purchasers can't get enough of that stock. The huge volume of price gaps is up, followed by significant profit-taking and a complete collapse in stock demand. Prices fall, and the trend significantly shifts.

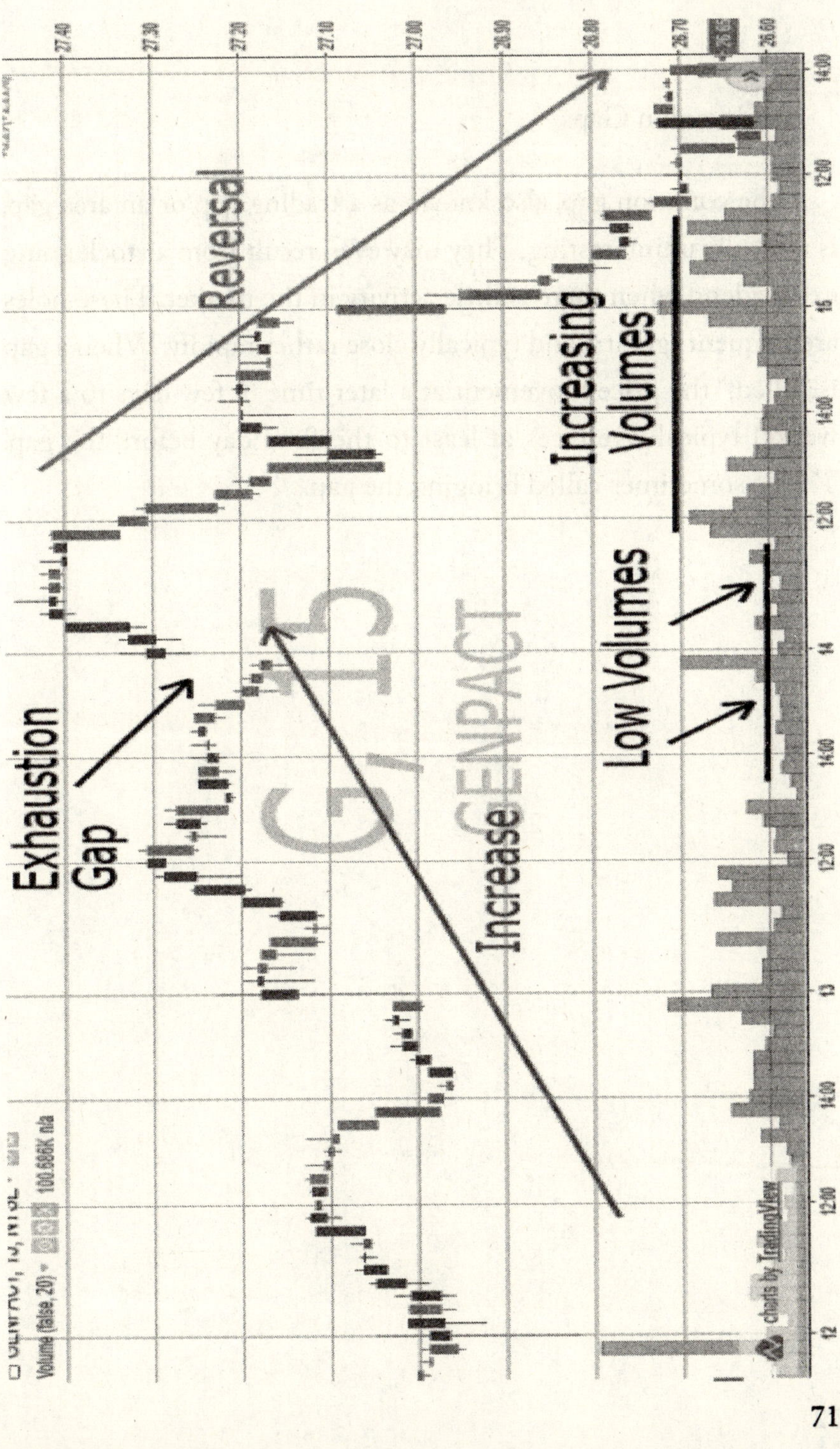
Exhaustion Gap
Reversal
Increase
Increasing Volumes
Low Volumes
GENPACT
charts by TradingView

4. Common Gaps

The common gap, also known as a trading gap or an area gap, is typically uninteresting. They may even result from a stock going ex-dividend when there is little activity in the market. These holes are frequent (get it?) and typically close rather rapidly. When a gap is "filled," the price movement at a later time (a few days to a few weeks) typically retraces at least to the final day before the gap. This is sometimes called bridging the gap.

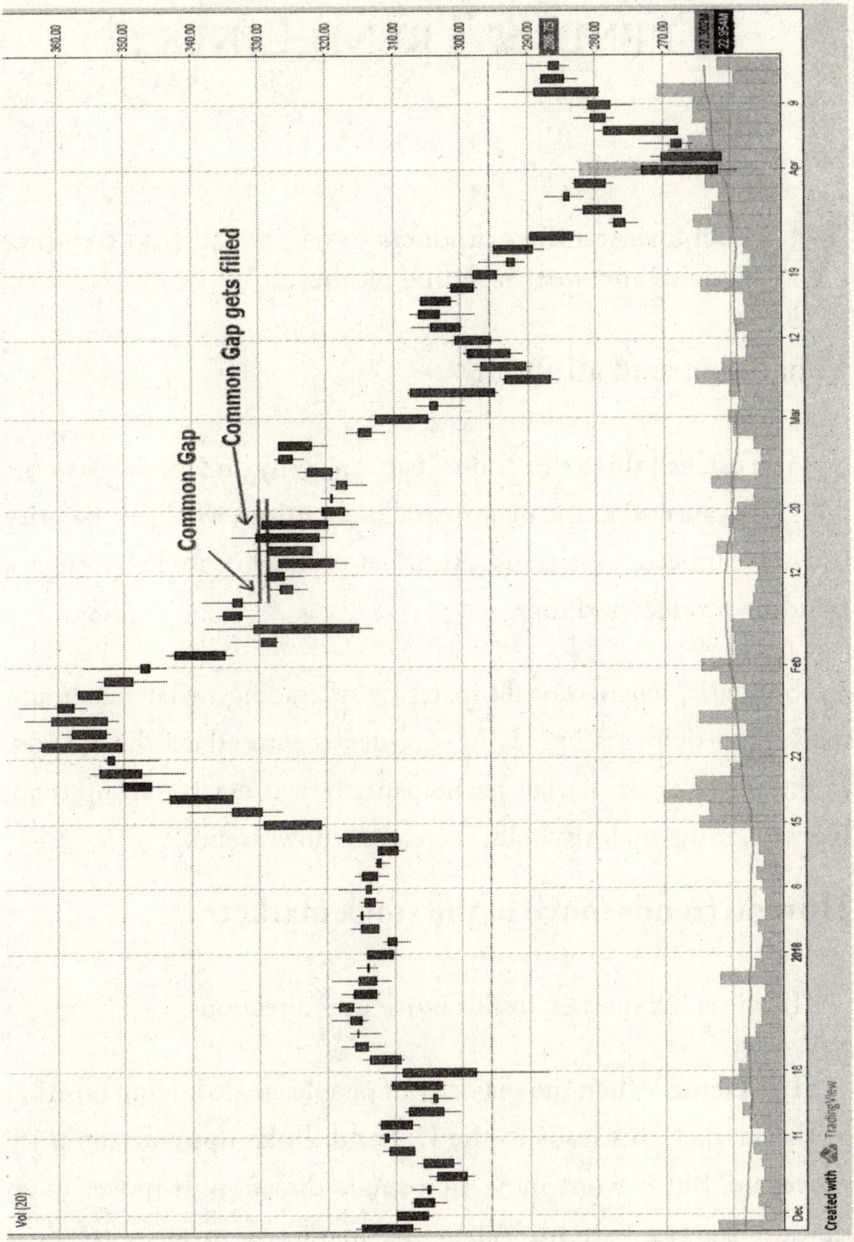

This is what common gap looks like on chart aligned with volume.

Trend & Trend Lines :

We all love trending products to use; we all read trending articles and wear trending clothes.

What is a trend all about?

You can call this a directional pattern. Why directional pattern? This is because what the majority talks about and what the majority use or wear becomes a trend. And that product or topic becomes a trending product and topic.

Similarly, when we talk in terms of trading, what maximum market participants are doing decides the trend of the market. If the majority of market participants buy, it creates an uptrend; likewise, if the majority sells, it creates a downtrend.

How do trends move in the stock market?

In the stock market, trends move in 3 directions:

UP Trend: When the majority of people create buying position in the market, this leads to the Uptrend. In an uptrend, the price moves up. But it won't move in a single direction. It moves in an upward zig-zag pattern. When the market is in an uptrend, it creates higher highs and higher lows.

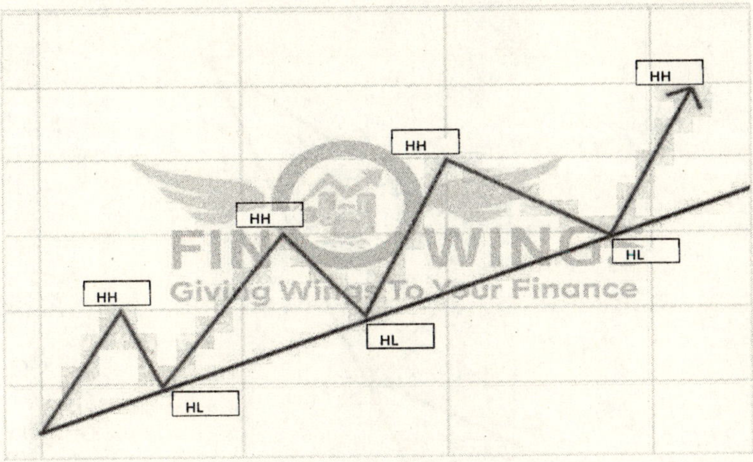

This how an Uptrend looks like. Notice that it is making Higher highs and Higher lows in the upward direction.

The line which connects the higher lows is called as Trend Line.

Trend breaks when price breaks the trend line and trades below the recent higher Low.

This shows that market participants are bullish and ready to buy the market every fall.

Down Trend: When the majority of people create a selling position in the market, this leads to the Downtrend. The reason could be anything like profit booking, bad news, bad government, or bad fundamentals. In a downtrend, the price moves down. But it won't move in a single direction. It moves in a downward zig-zag pattern. When the market is in a downtrend, it creates Lower highs and lower lows.

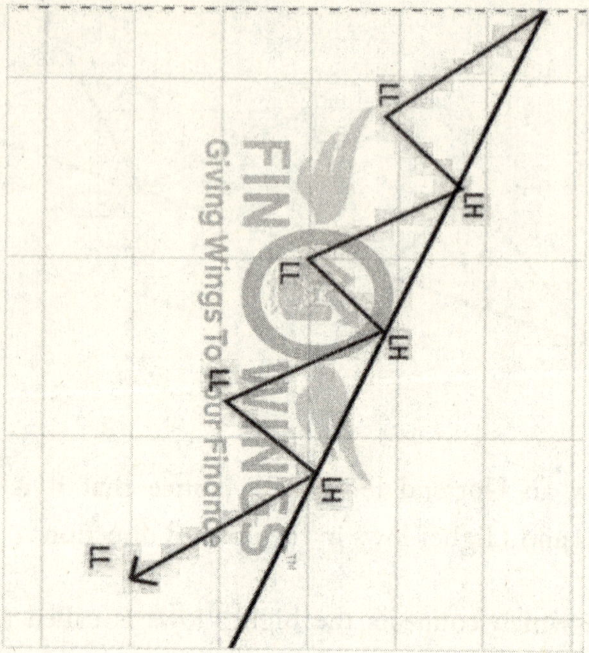

This how a Downtrend looks like. Notice that it is making Lower highs and Lower lows in the downward direction.

The line which connects the Lower Highs is called as Trend Line.

Trend lines increase the visibility of trends and make it easy to identify the trend and trend breakout.

Trend breaks if price breaks the trend line and starts trading above the recent lower high.

Side Ways: This shows the confusion in the market. In which buyers and sellers are trading in a range, therefore no directional trend forms. This kind of market is also called a choppy market. During this market, we are confused about where to move Up or Down.

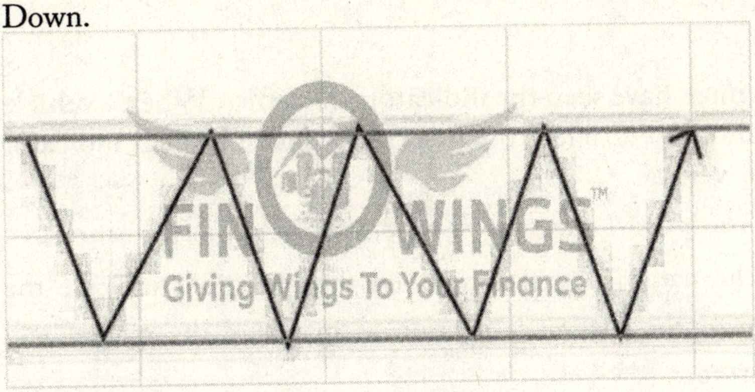

This is what a sideways market looks like. Many investors and traders avoid this phase of the market and decide not to trade. The best way to trade this type of market is by Buying at the bottom and selling at the top of the range.

Indicators

You must have seen the indicators in traffics. When a vehicle is about to turn left, the rider starts showing a left indicator and vice-versa.

As the name suggests, these are the tools that indicate the direction of the market. Direction as in where the market will move further?

An indicator is a technical tool that uses the price and indicates the view of the market and also tries to predict the future move of the market; these views are based on statistical calculation.

In this book, I am going to deal with the most important indicator which works well and is most often used.

Moving Average: It is the most common and most used indicator in stock trading. You will hardly find anyone who doesn't have any average line on this chart. It is just a normal average of prices of the different time intervals. Like if you want to see the average price for the past ten days, you need to calculate the average of the past ten day's price. But on the chart, you do not need to plot anything. You will get all the indicators on your charting tools.

Two most used moving averages in the stock market:

Simple Moving Average : As its name suggest, it is just a simple moving average. The formula would be: The closing price of the past ten days divided by 20, this will give you the 20-day average closing price of the market.

Exponential Moving Average : The main difference between both the averages is that the Simple Moving average gives equal weight to the entire price, but the exponential moving average gives more weight to the recent price. Calculation of EMA is quite tricky, but don't worry; you don't need to calculate this, but you should know the process.

To calculate the EMA, first, find the simple moving average of 20 days, and after that, calculate the multiplier to give more weight to the EMA; this is known as the "smoothing factor." The formula to find the smoothing factor is (2 divided by time period +1). Use the multiplier 2 for 20 moving average. Then add the smoothing factor with yesterday's EMA; this will give the value of today's EMA.

EMAt = [Vt * (s/1+d)] + EMAy * [1-(s/1+d)]

In this formula,

EMAt = Today's EMA

Vt = Value Today

EMAy = Yesterday's EMA

s = Smoothing factor

d= No. of days.

I know it's quite difficult to understand, but don't worry, as I said, you don't need to calculate.

Traders generally use a combination of moving averages like 9 and 21 for intraday or swing trading, 50 and 100 for positional trading, and 200 for long-term investment.

Moving averages also act as dynamic support and resistance.

You can use a combination of 20, 50, 100, and 200 moving averages, in which 20 will work as a short-term or intraday trend decider, 50 and 100 for swing and position, and 200 acts as major support and resistance in the long term.

When the price is above the average, it indicates an uptrend, and if it trades below the moving average, it indicates a downtrend.

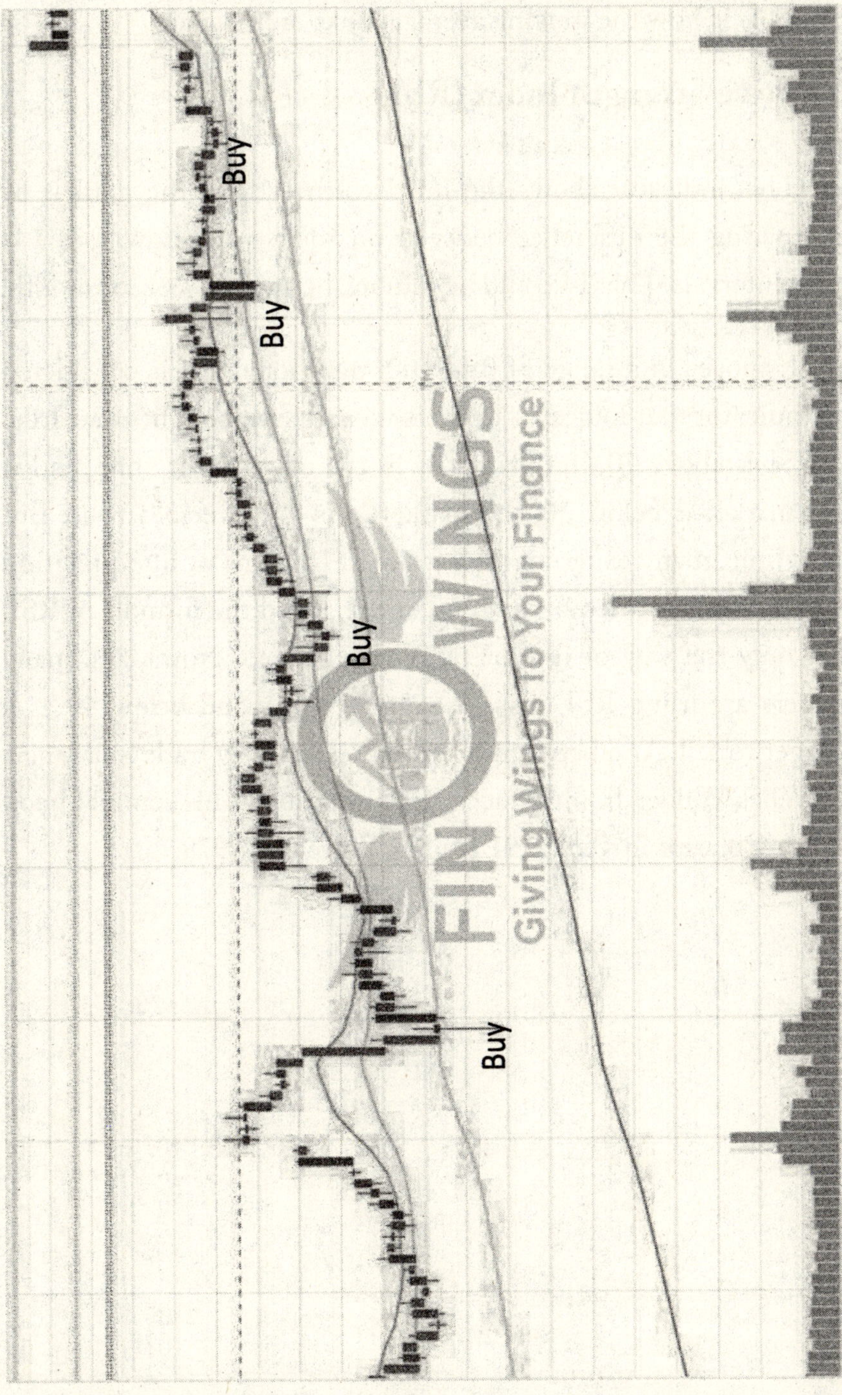
Buy
Buy
Buy
Buy

This is how the moving average looks on the chart.

Relative Strength Index (RSI)

This indicator shows the relative strength of the market by comparing the difference between no. of ups and downs in 14-time intervals. This 14 could be minute, hour, day, week, or month.

It moves in a range of 0 to 100; traditionally, it is considered an indicator that indicates an oversold and over-bought zone. Like if RSI is above 70, the market is in the overbought zone, and if the market is below 30, the market is in the oversold zone. But over time, many experiments happened in terms of interpretation of RSI levels. Remember that no one changed the formula of RSI, but only the way of interpretation is changed. Nowadays, many traders are using RSI 60 as a trigger to buy and below 40 as a trigger to sell. And between 60 – 40 markets may trade in a range. J. Welles Wilder Jr. introduced this indicator in his seminal book "New Concept in Technical Trading Systems," 1978.

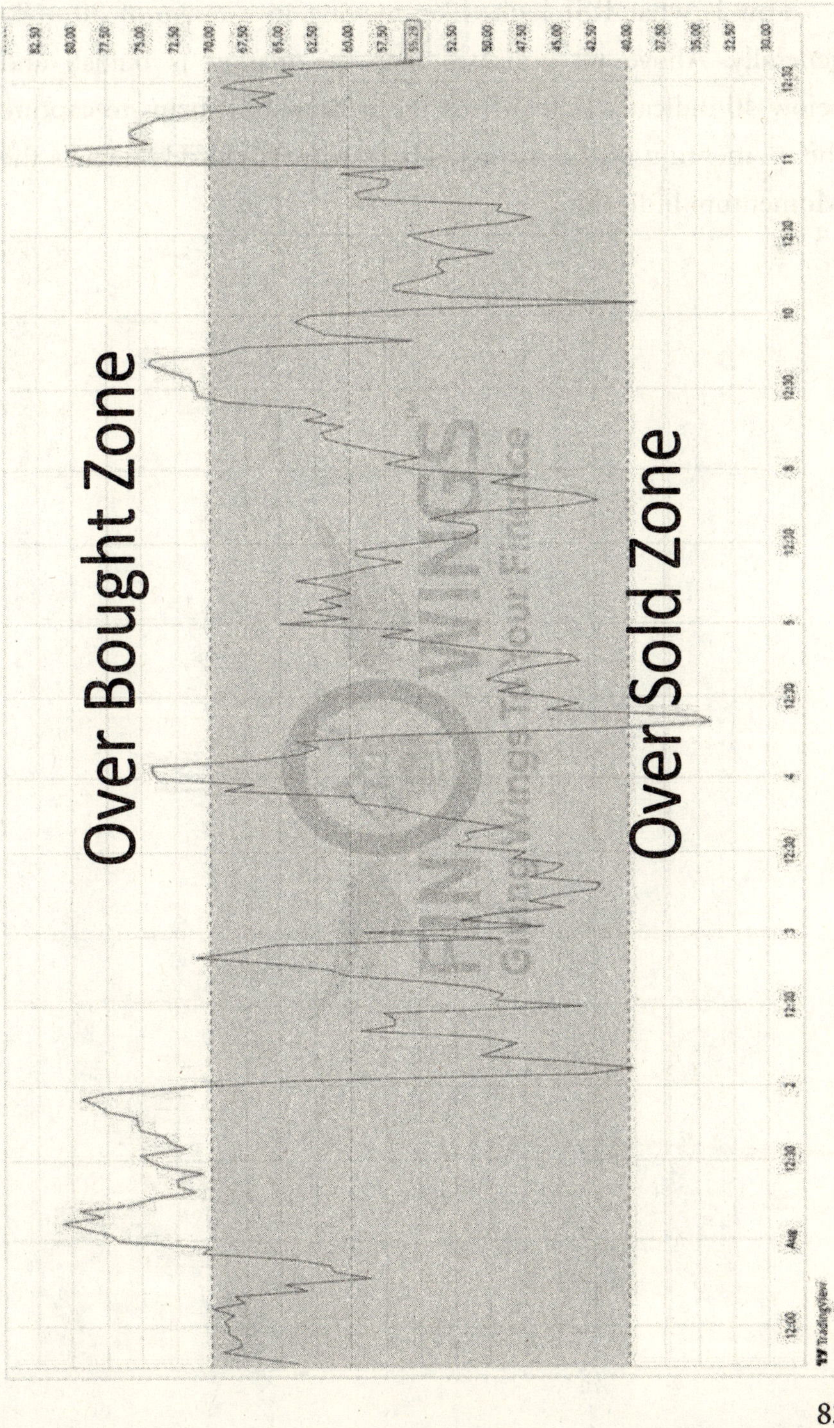
Over Bought Zone
Over Sold Zone

This is what RSI looks like, moving in a range of 30 – 80 generally. Above 60 indicates that the market is bullish and below 40 indicates that the market is bearish. It helps to capture the momentum of the market. That's why it is also known as the Momentum indicator.

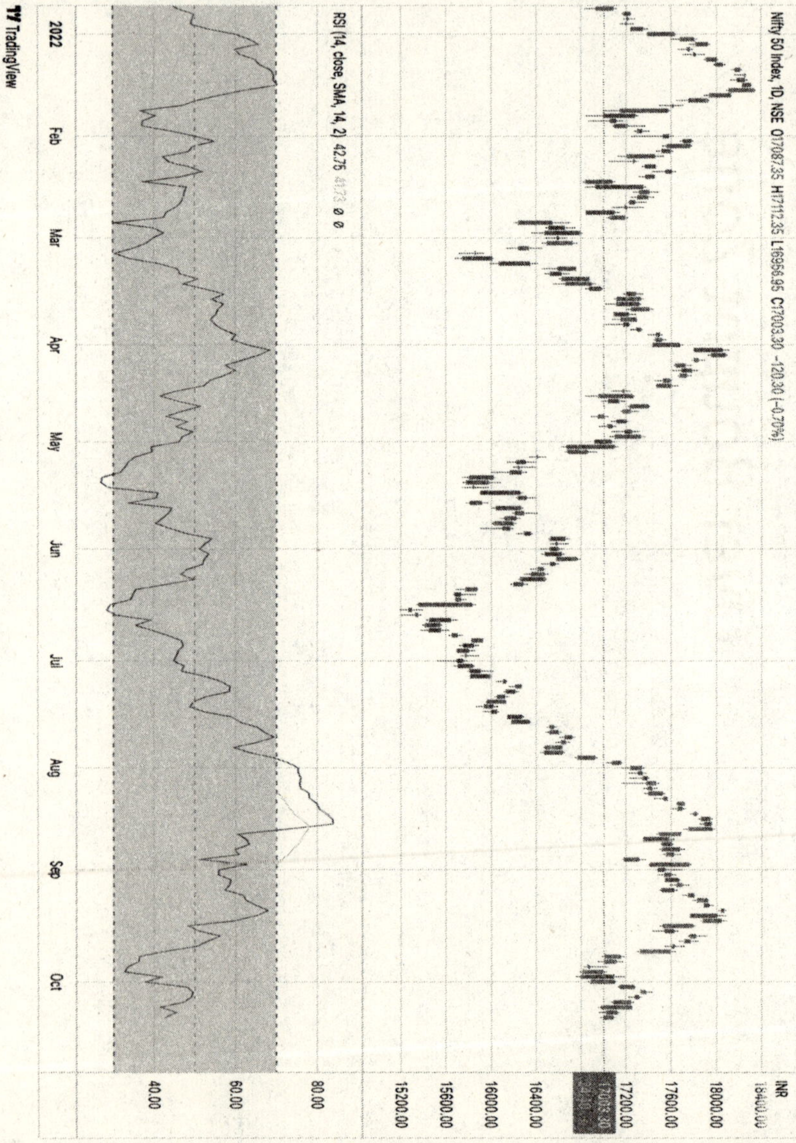

Let's summarise RSI in bullet points for you.

Overbought and oversold conditions are indicated by the RSI being above 70 and below 30, respectively. These standard levels can also be modified if necessary to better meet security requirements. For instance, if security is continuously getting close to the overbought level of 70, you might want to boost this level to 80.

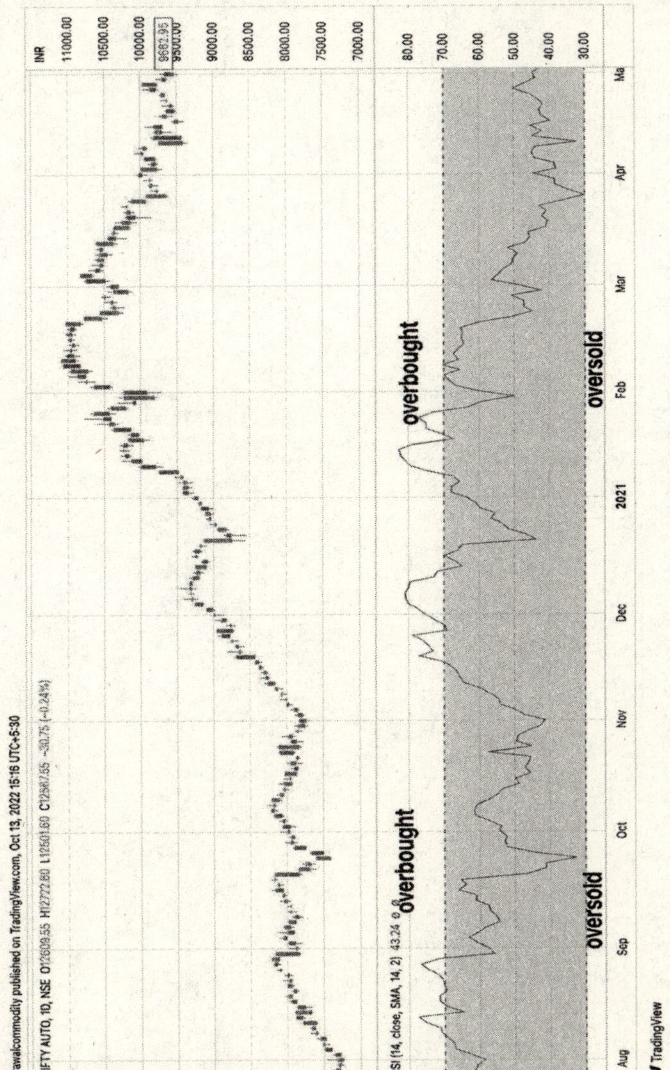

Additionally, the RSI regularly generates chart patterns, such as double tops and bottoms and trend lines, which may not be visible on the underlying price chart. On the RSI, keep an eye out for resistance or support.

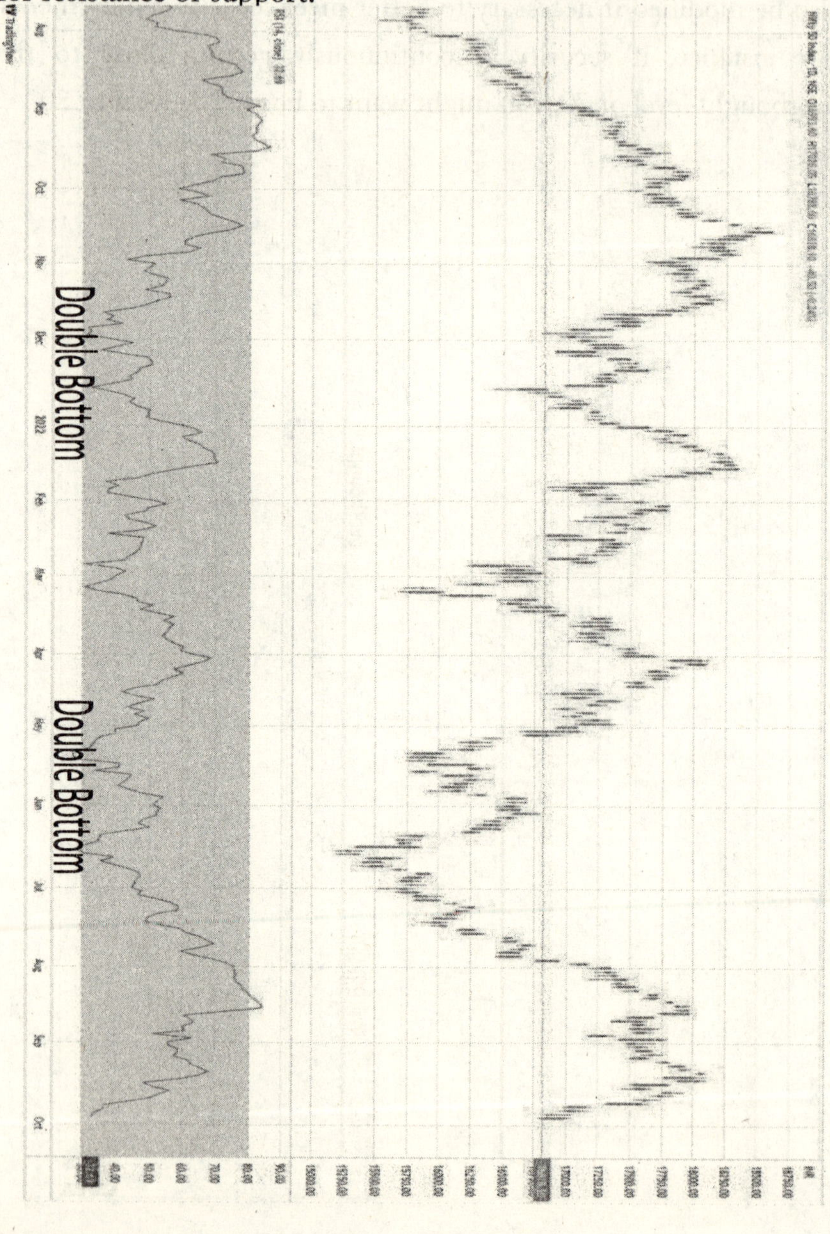

- During an uptrend or bull market, the RSI normally oscillates between 40 and 90, with the 40-50 region acting as support.

- During a fall or bear market, the RSI normally oscillates between 10 and 60, with the 50–60 range acting as resistance.

- Based on the RSI characteristics and the strength of the underlying trend for the securities or market, these ranges may fluctuate.

- The divergence can indicate a price reversal if the underlying prices hit a new high or low that isn't supported by the RSI.

- A top swing failure happens if the RSI makes a lower high followed by a downside move below a prior low.

- A bottom swing failure happens if the RSI makes a higher low and then follows with an upward movement above a prior high.

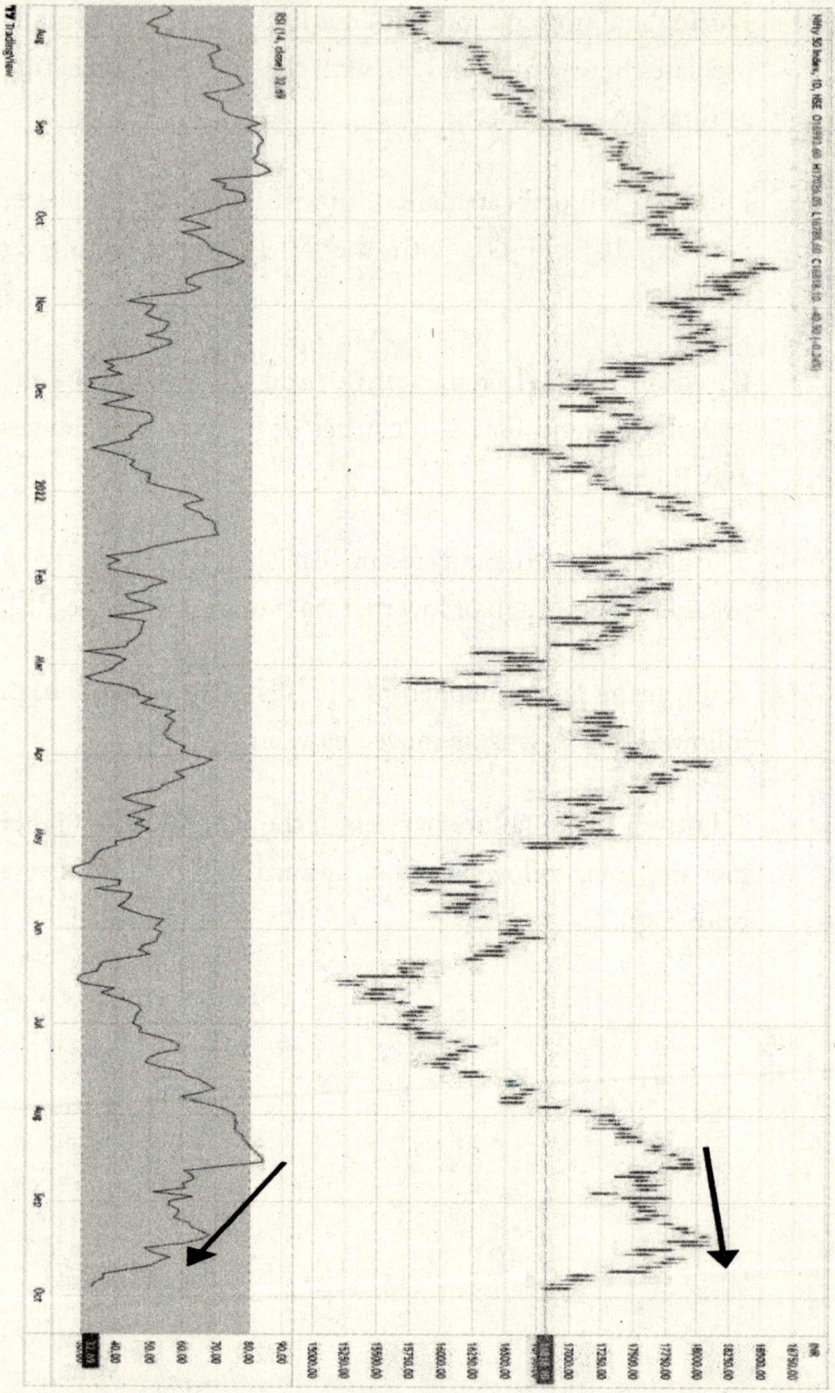

MACD (Moving Average Convergence Divergence)-

This indicator works well in the trending market. It just indicates the relation between 12 periods EMA and 26 periods EMA. You need to subtract the 26 EMA from the 12 EMA; this will give you the MACD line, also known as a baseline.

After, you need to calculate nine days EMA of the MACD line, which we call the "Signal Line." When MACD moves above the signal line, it indicates a buy signal, and when it moves below the signal line, it indicates a sell signal.

When 12 EMA is above the 26 EMA, this gives the positive MACD, which is also an indication of buy.

When 12 EMA is below the 26 EMA, this gives the negative MACD, which is an indication of Sell.

In some charting tools, you will also find a histogram in MACD; these histograms represent the distance between the MACD line and the signal line. When the histogram is above the baseline, it indicates a bullish view, and when the histogram is below the baseline, it indicates a bearish view.

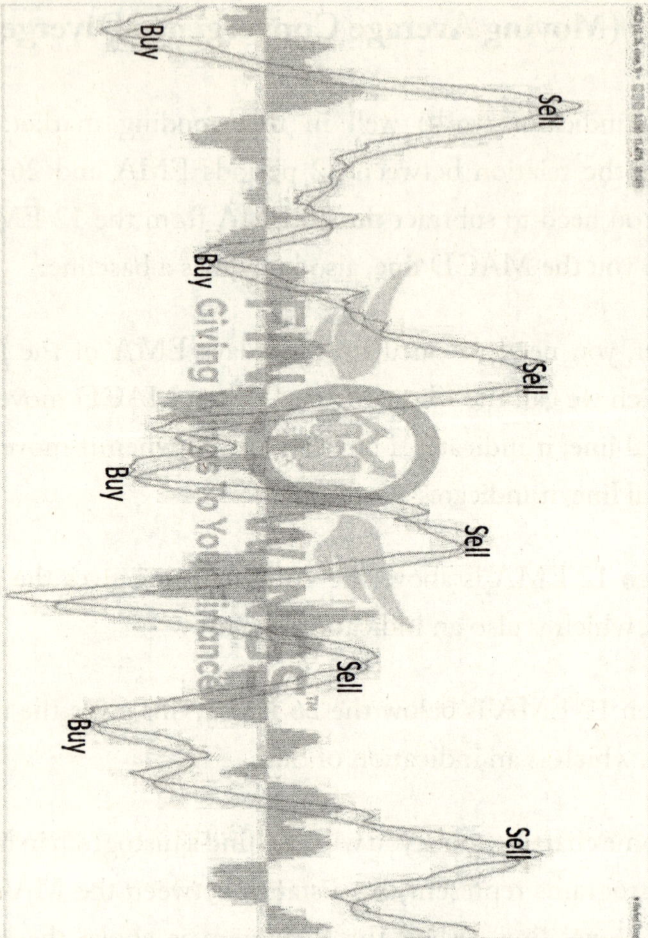

This is how MACD looks on the chart. MACD above the signal line triggers buy signals, and MACD below the Signal line trigger sell signals. I'll discuss the use of MACD in detail in the coming chapters so that you can relate easily.

These are the technical indicators that are used by most traders.

You must check and try these indicators, do let me know how it worked for you.

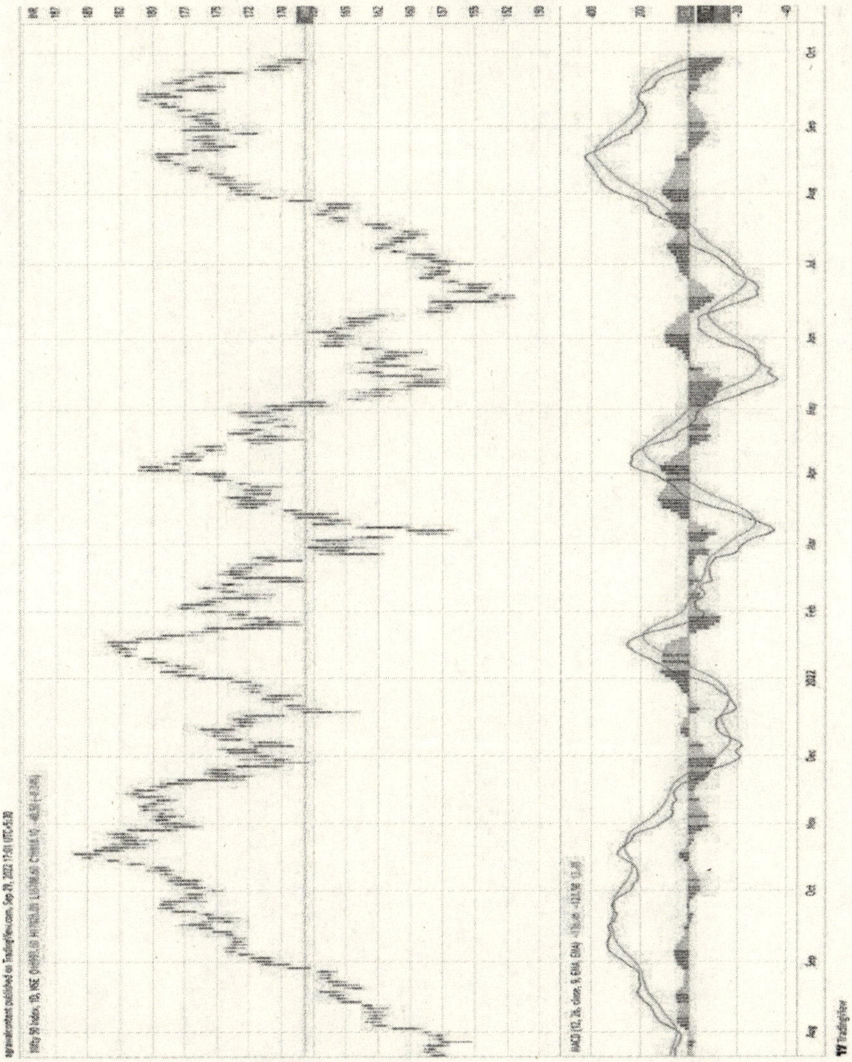

Let's summarise the MACD:

Crossing the MACD above zero is bullish, and crossing it below zero is bearish. Second, it is bullish when the MACD turns up from below zero. A downward turn from above zero is regarded as bearish.

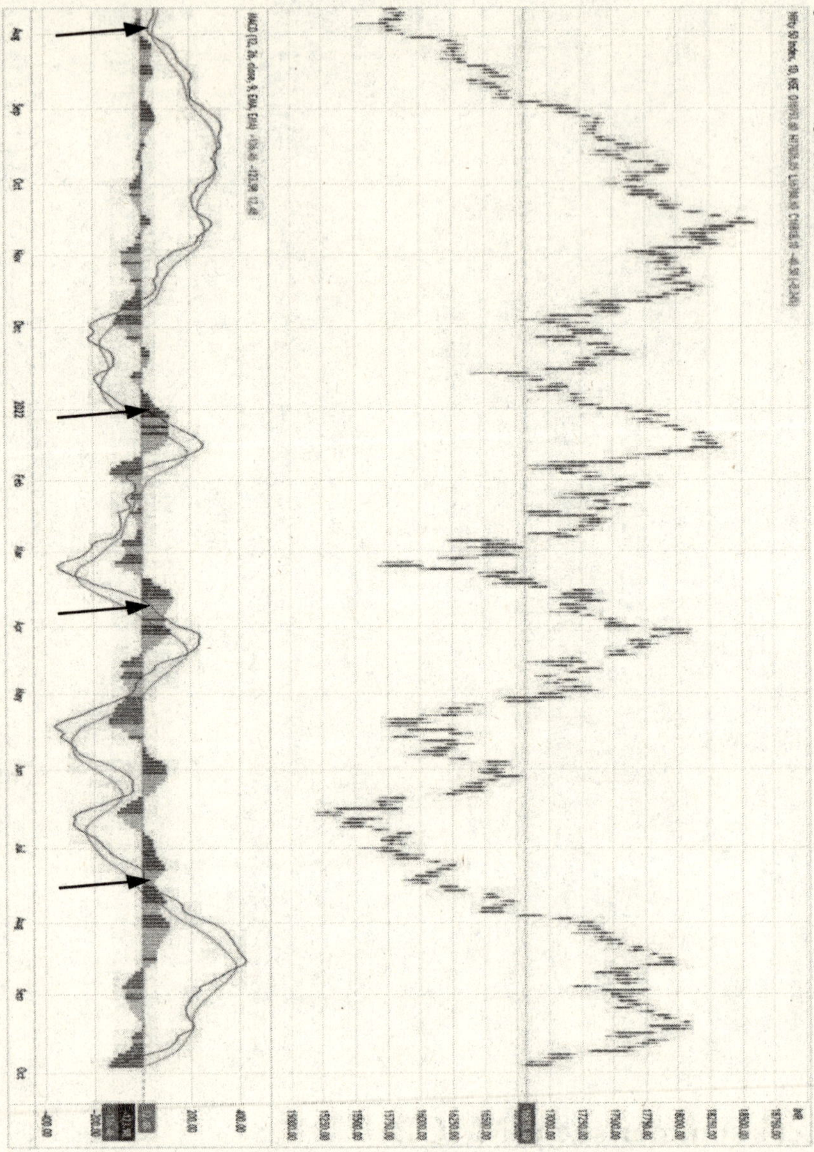

- The MACD line is seen as bullish when it crosses over the signal line from below. The signal gets stronger the deeper below the zero line it is.

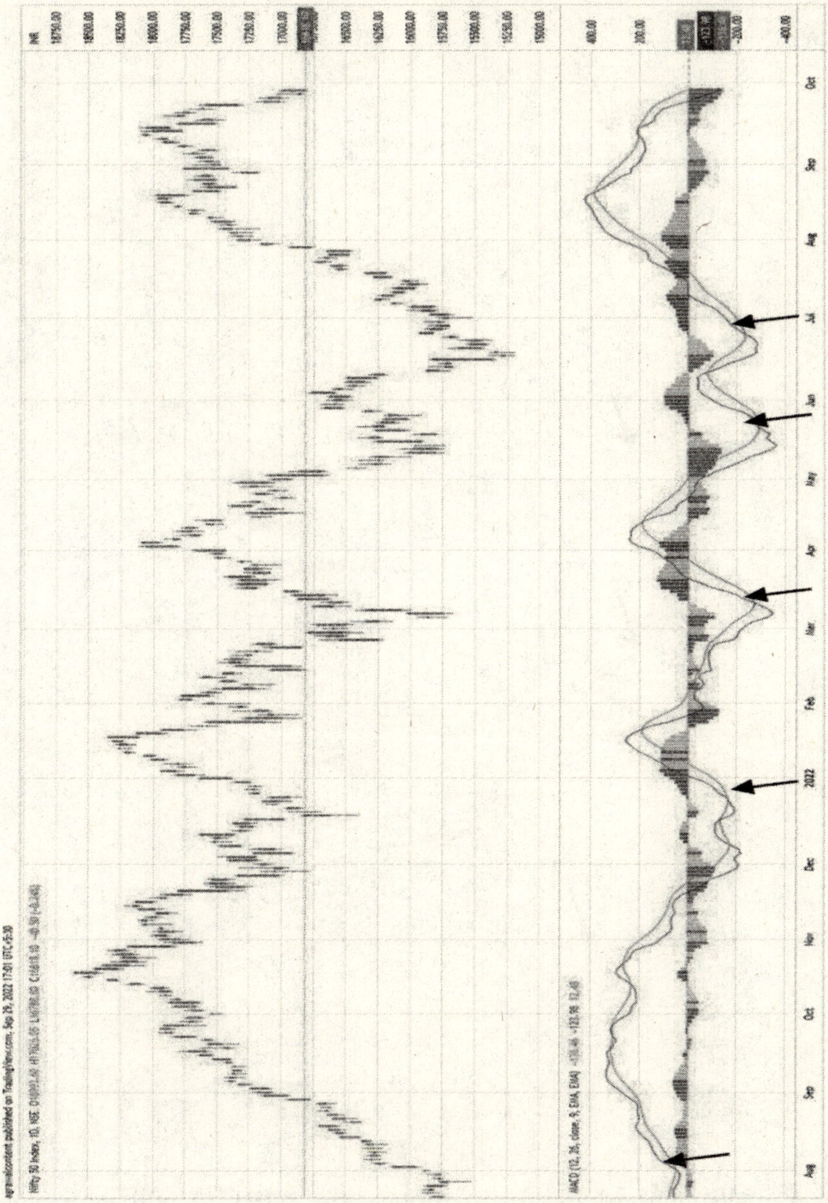

- The MACD line is seen as bearish when it crosses from above to below the signal line.

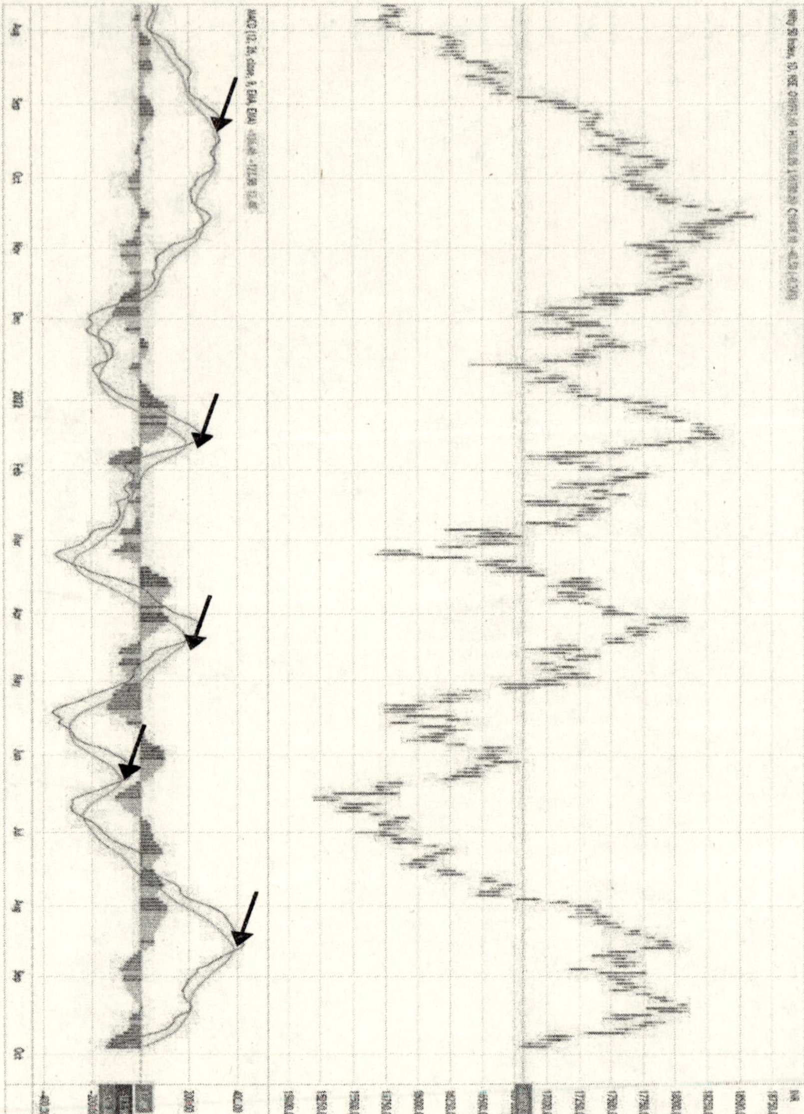

- When markets are in ranges, the MACD will whipsaw, with the fast line crossing the signal line repeatedly. When faced with this scenario, MACD users typically steer clear of trading or close out positions to lower portfolio volatility.

- When it confirms the crossing indications, the divergence between the MACD and the price action is a stronger indicator.

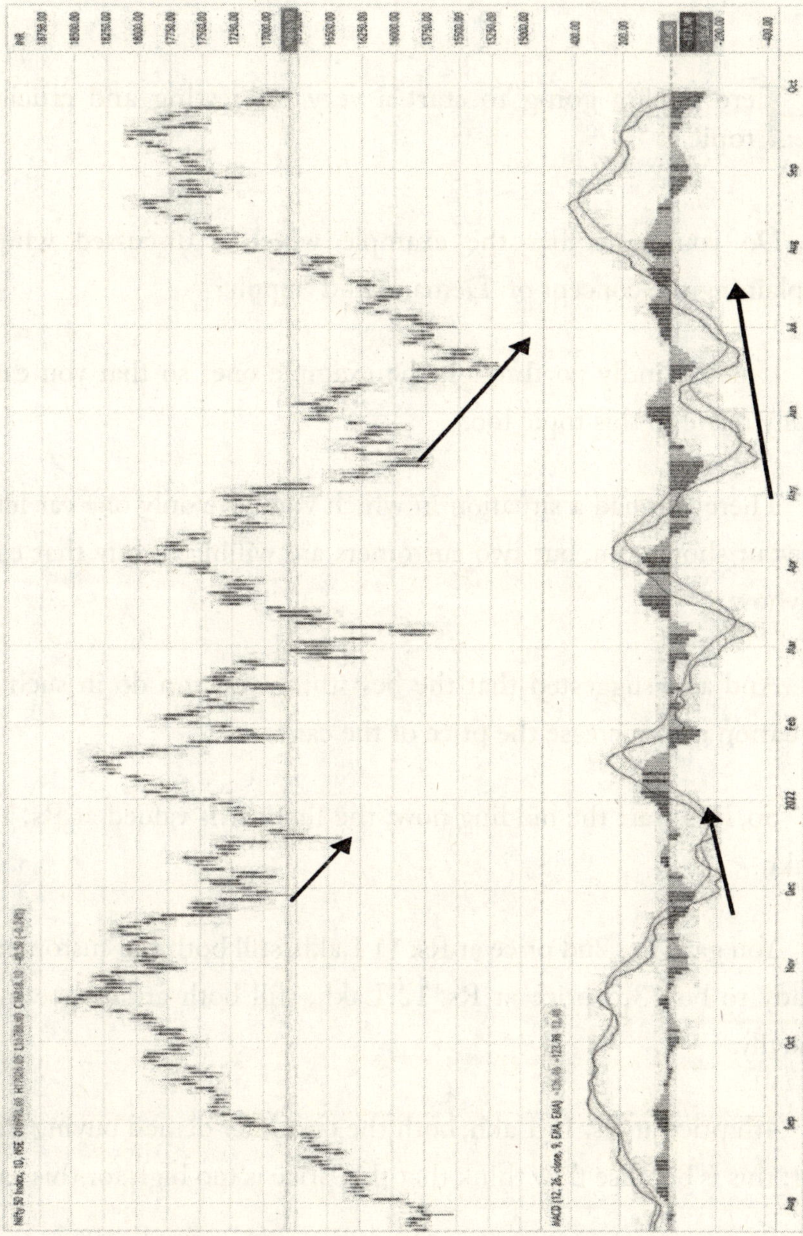

Resistance and Support

Here we are going to start a very interesting and crucial topic.

Do you remember the example which I discussed while explaining the concept of Demand and Supply?

If not! Kindly go through the example ones so that you can easily relate to this topic too.

There you had a situation in which you have only one car left in your showroom, but two customers are willing to buy that car anyhow.

And as I suggested that the best thing you can do in such a situation is to increase the price of the car.

So, let's start the bidding now; the first car is valued at Rs. 10 Lakh.

You gave the 2nd price at Rs. 11 Lakh, still both the customers ready to buy. 3rd price at Rs. 12 Lakh, still both are competing equally.

4th price at Rs. 15 Lakh, both the customer denied buying the car; this is because they think that this price is too high for this car.

Let's understand what happened here; both the customer wanted to buy the car and was ready to pay the price as per the real value of the car. But after increasing the price of the car at a certain level, both were ready to buy, but at a point of Rs. 15 Lakh, both stepped out of the deal.

In that case Rs. 15 Lakh act as a resistance price for the customer above which they can't afford to buy or maybe not to value the product at that price. It shows that at the resistance level, buyers are not active. Therefore, we can say that resistance is the point at which buyers are not willing to buy, so the sellers have to reduce the price, which leads to a fall in price. We can also say this point is a supply point.

Because at this level buyers are not interested so in selling the product, sellers have to reduce the price.

In terms of technical analysis, we can say that resistance is the point at which traders and investors are not willing to buy the shares, which leads to a fall in the price of the share.

When the price of the shares rises, it rises till its resistance point after it approaches the low side, where buyers find this underpriced and ready to buy again.

One more important point to note is that if somehow resistance breaks, this may indicate a big move in the market in the near future; this is because breaking the point where buyers are not ready to buy means there should be some valid reason which may lead the market at the different resistance level.

Price rally in a bull market, during this rally resistance, tells us that price will rise up to which point.

Technically it shows the upside level, like where the price may reach further. Therefore, you can say that resistance is the point at or above which market participants are not willing to buy the shares, so the price of the share may fall from the resistance point.

Now just turn the situation, as of now you as a car showroom owner giving the price because you got excess demand.

But as you have increased the price of the car, both customers denied buying the car.

What will be the next step in that case?

You need to reduce the price, in order to hold at least one of the customers. But at this time, power shifted in the customer's hand.

Customers start breaking the price down because they observe that now your willingness to sell the car is more than their willingness to buy the car.

They quoted Rs. 9 Lakh for the car, but as per you, it will be a loss-making deal if you sell the car below Rs. 10 Lakh. So, you decided to stick at Rs. 10 Lakh.

After some time, one of the customers decided not to buy the car, because he wanted to pay only Rs. 9 Lakh, so he moved out of the showroom. But one customer is still in the showroom and waiting to get a better deal from you. But you made a clear point that you will not sell the car below Rs. 10 Lakh.

Now, let's understand the situation carefully and what you actually did; you supported the price to not move below Rs. 10 Lakh. That is what we call a support point.

Where market participants are not willing to sell below that and the buyer has to buy at this level.

When the market is in a Downtrend, the price will fall but where it falls is the support point. Below, which sellers are not ready to sell, or you can also say that at that point, buyers are happily ready to buy. It might be because buyers found that level at the right price. The reason could be anything. But the point supported is the point at which the price stops falling and may rise from that point.

This is what support on the chart looks like.

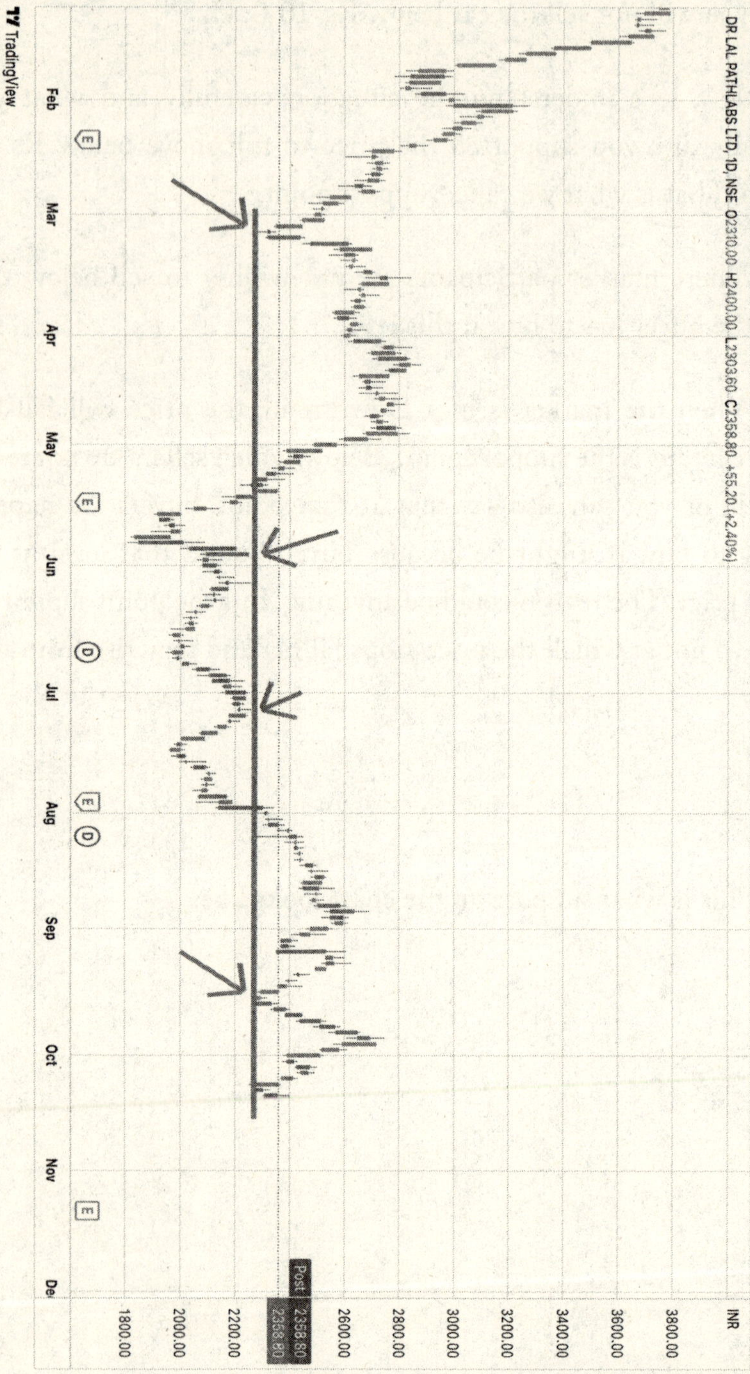
agrawalcommodity published on TradingView.com, Oct 13, 2022 15:52 UTC+5:30
DR LAL PATHLABS LTD, 1D, NSE O2310.00 H2400.00 L2303.60 C2358.80 +55.20 (+2.40%)
INR
3800.00
3600.00
3400.00
3200.00
3000.00
2800.00
2600.00
2358.80
2200.00
2000.00
1800.00
Feb
Mar
Apr
May
Jun
Jul
Aug
Sep
Oct
Nov
Dec
TradingView

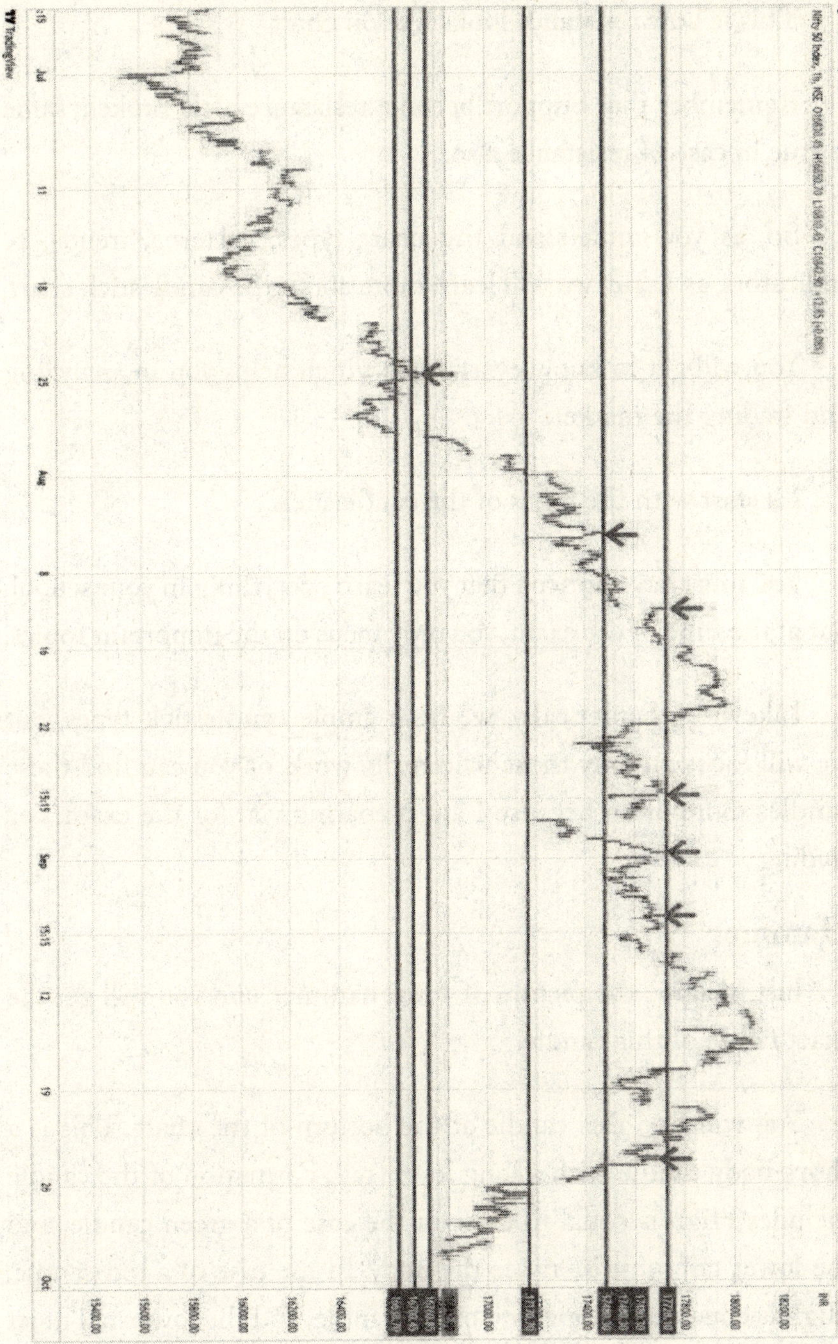

This is how resistance looks like on chart.

Remember that Support become resistance after broken, same is true in case of resistance also.

So, as you understand the chart types, patterns, trends, & indicators, as I said, we will learn more about the candlestick chart.

You will get to know everything which helps you in analyzing and trading the market.

I'll start with the types of the candlestick.

You must have noticed that you learn everything in your school, but at the time of the exam, you only focus on the important topics.

Likewise, theoretically, we have ample candlestick types, but we will focus on only those who really work, or you can find these candles more often because I am preparing you for the exam, i.e., trading.

Hammer

Just imagine the picture of a real hammer, and you will get the exact figure of this candle.

You will find this candle at the bottom of the chart. This is a short-body candle with a long lower tail. Formation of the candle includes High is equal to close in the case of a green candle, and the lower tail must be twice the body. In the case of a red candle, High is equal to the opening of the candle, and the lower tail must be twice the body.

See the figure below:

This is what a hammer looks like, exactly the same as a real hammer. Try to understand the psychology behind the candle, Market khula 100 pe, nichey gaya 50 tk, but fir buyers aaye or market ko 50 sey 125 tk le gaye and 125 pe hi market close hua.

What does this show? Who is in Power? Bulls or Bears? Buyers or Sellers?

It is clear that bears took the market at 50 from 100; this shows the dominancy of bears at the beginning of the market starts.

But after that, bulls pulled the market back towards the day high and took the market to 125 from the Low of 50 and also able to close near the day high.

Bears imposed the power of 50 points but were not able to hold the position, and bulls imposed the power of 75 points from the low and also held the market at a high level.

This shows that bulls are dominating the bears.

You will get this candle at the bottom only. So, if bulls are trying to dominate bears at the bottom level, it indicates that the market may reverse from this level. That is why the hammer is considered a reversal candle. It shows the sign of reversal.

A few things you need to keep in mind are: Hammer only works if found in the bottom. Colour is not very important in this candle.

The tail of the candle should be at least twice the body.

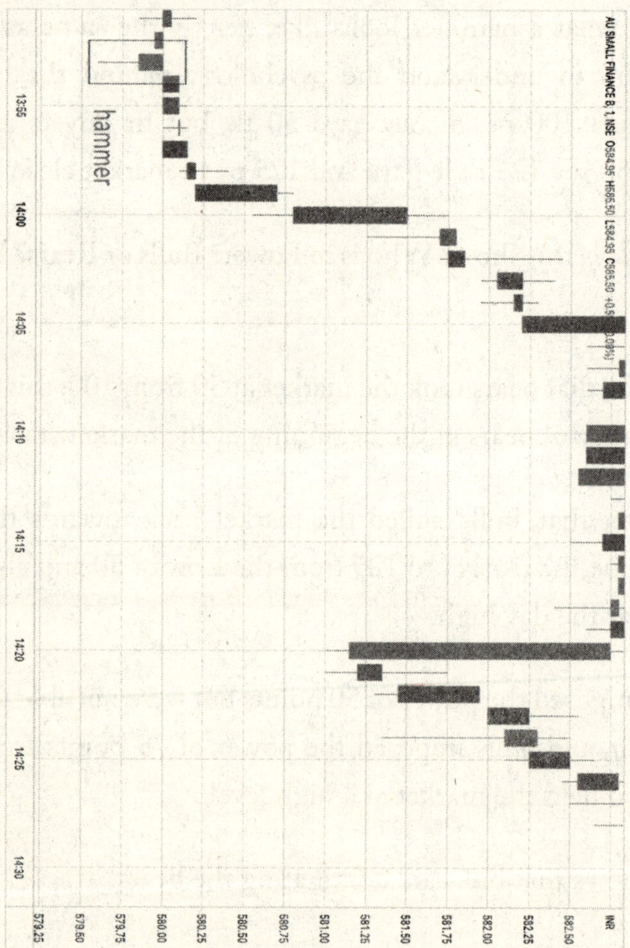

See the picture above, you will find the hammer at the bottom, and after the hammer, you will see a reversal as seen in the figure. This shows that after the continuous fall, buyers are ready to take charge now.

One should consider taking a long position above the high of the hammer, with the Stop Loss of low of the candle.

Inverted Hammer

Just reverse the hammer; this candle is also found at the bottom. The shape is also similar to a hammer, but the psychology is quite different. This is a short-body candle with a long higher tail.

Formation of the candle includes Low is equal to open in case of green candle, and higher tail must be twice of the body. In the case of a red candle, Low is equal to the close of the candle, and the higher tail must be twice the body.

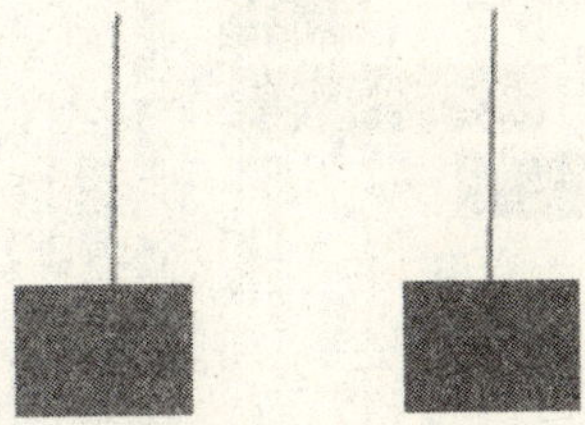

This is what an inverted hammer looks like..

Let's see on chart:

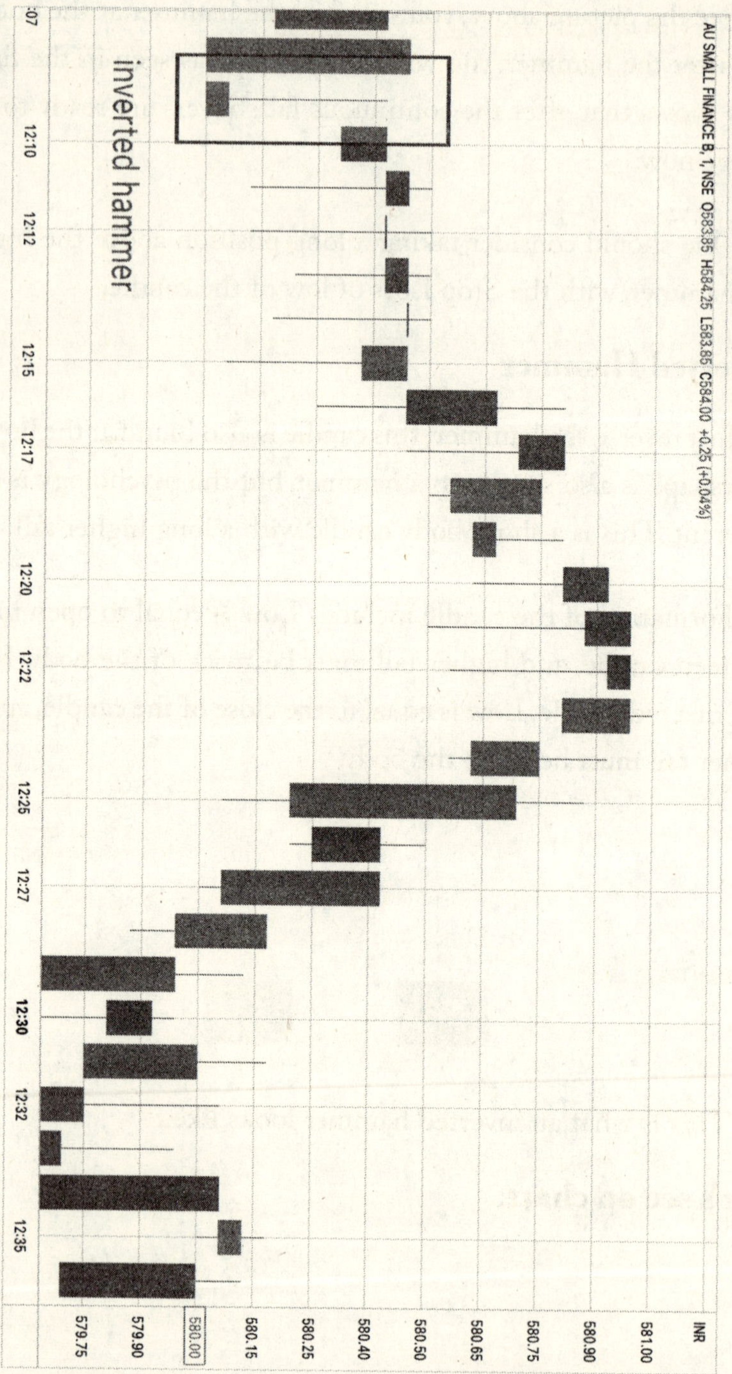
agrawalcommodity published on TradingView.com, Oct 13, 2022 14:48 UTC+5:30
AU SMALL FINANCE B, 1, NSE O583.85 H584.25 L583.85 C584.00 +0.25 (+0.04%)
inverted hammer
INR
581.00
580.90
580.75
580.65
580.50
580.40
580.25
580.15
580.00
579.90
579.75
:07
12:10
12:12
12:15
12:17
12:20
12:22
12:25
12:27
12:30
12:32
12:35
TradingView

As you can see, there is an inverted hammer at the bottom; after continuous fall, bulls try to take charge, that's price rises too high, but because of continuous fall, market participants are also less confident in taking long positions. That's why the price is sustained at the high. But it shows that bulls might take charge soon. That's why this is also considered a bullish reversal candle.

It gives double confirmation if formed after the hammer. It means you can be more confident when you find a hammer and an inverted hammer at the bottom. In this situation, traders can create a long position above the high of the inverted hammer, with the Stop Loss of low of the hammer.

You should take care of the positioning of the candles. It matters a lot. Hammer and inverted hammer only work well if found at the bottom or at support.

What if you found a hammer and an inverted hammer at the top? Everything like shape, color, and psychology remains the same, but the name and interpretation will change.

Hanging Man

When a hammer is found at the top, it is called a Hanging Man. Because it looks like a man hanging at the top and ready to fall, the shape formation of the candle will be the same as a hammer. So, let's not waste time on repeated information. Let's jump directly to the chart and see how to trade this candle.

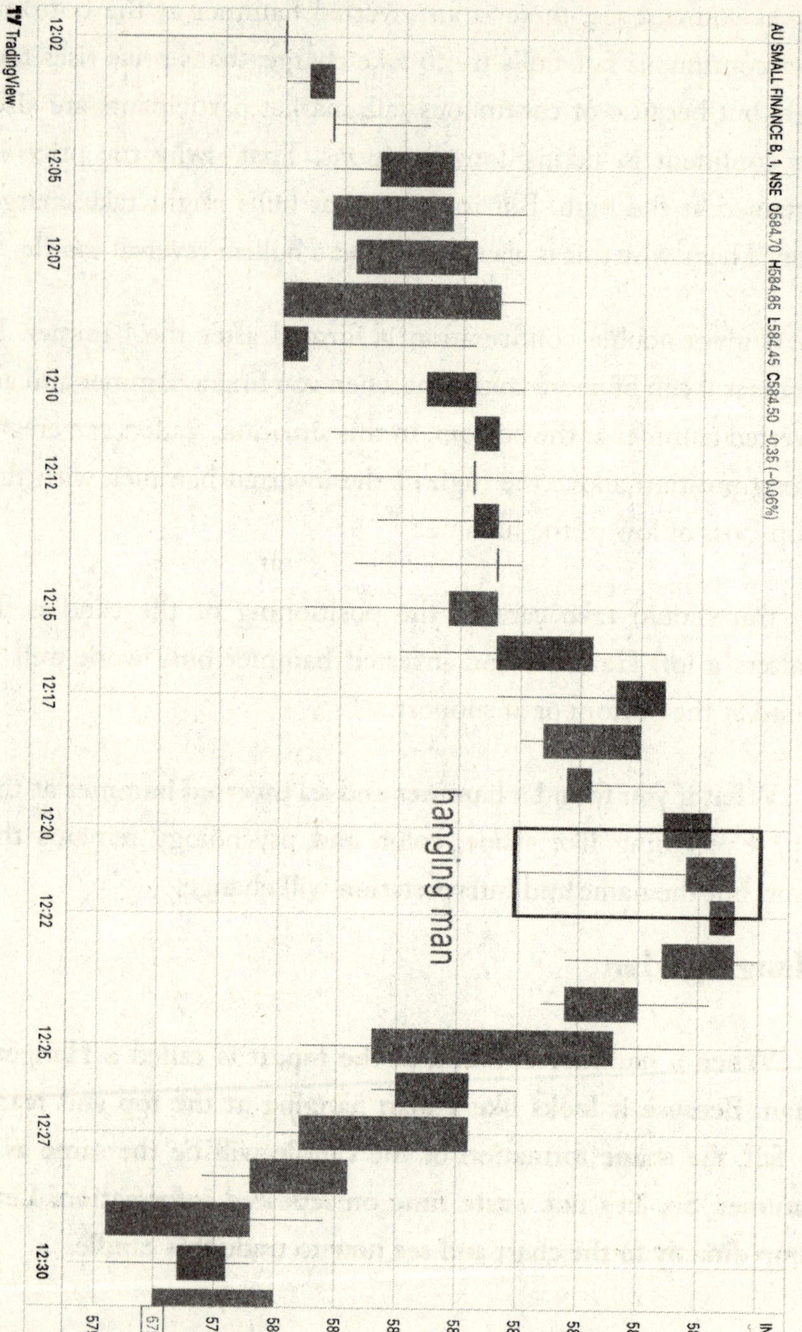
agrawalcommodity published on TradingView.com, Oct 13, 2022 14:47 UTC+5:30
AU SMALL FINANCE B, 1, NSE O584.70 H584.86 L584.45 C584.50 −0.35 (−0.06%)
hanging man
INR
580.90
580.75
580.65
580.50
580.40
580.25
580.15
580.00
579.90
579.75
579.65
12:02
12:05
12:07
12:10
12:12
12:15
12:17
12:20
12:22
12:25
12:27
12:30
TradingView

As you can see in the figure above, a hanging man is always found at the top of the rally or near resistance; this shows that after the continuous rally, bears try to take charge, which leads to the formation of the long lower tail. Hence, it gives the sign of bearish reversal. Traders can take the short position below the Low of the hanging man, with a stop loss of high of the hanging man.

Shooting Star

Just like a hammer and hanging man, the shooting star is also similar to an inverted hammer. Colour and psychology remain the same, but the name and interpretation will change.

When an inverted hammer is found at the top, it is called a Shooting Star. Because it looks like a shooting Star at the top, which is ready to fall, the shape formation of the candle will be the same as an inverted hammer. So, let's not waste time on repeated information. Let's jump directly to the chart and see how to trade this candle.

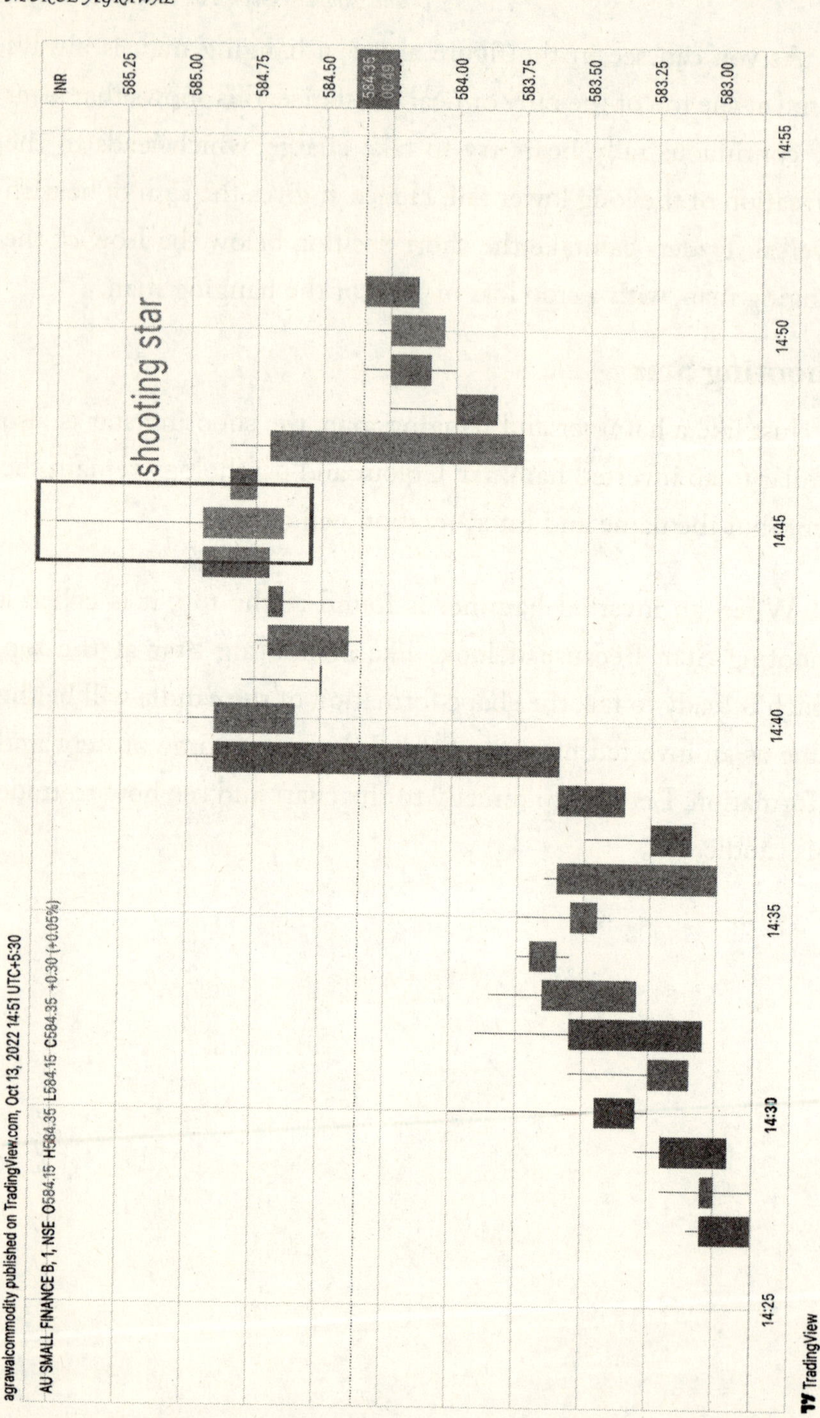
agrawalcommodity published on TradingView.com, Oct 13, 2022 14:51 UTC+5:30
AU SMALL FINANCE B, 1, NSE O584.15 H584.35 L584.15 C584.35 +0.30 (+0.05%)
shooting star
INR
585.25
585.00
584.75
584.50
584.00
583.75
583.50
583.25
583.00
14:25
14:30
14:35
14:40
14:45
14:50
14:55
TradingView

As you can see in the figure, a shooting star is found at the top of the rally or near resistance. Like hanging man, this candle also shows that the market might reverse. After a continuous rally, bears tried to take charge, which leads a fall in the market. Hence, this candle is also considered a reversal candle.

Traders can take a short position below the low of shooting start, with the Stop Loss of high of the shooting star.

So, if I try to summarize the four candles type which I talked about till now. It's basically a hammer only, the thinking process remains the same, but the positioning of the candle makes the interpretation different, which triggers the trade further.

Found hammer at the bottom can go long above the high of the hammer with the SL of the Low of the hammer.

Found inverted hammer at the bottom, Can go long above the high of the inverted hammer with the SL of the Low of the inverted hammer.

Found hanging man at the top, can go short below the Low of the hanging man with the SL of high of the hanging man.

Found shooting star at the top, can go short below the Low of the shooting star with the SL of high of the shooting star.

Engulfing Candle

This candle is considered both reversal and a continuous candle. It works exactly as its name. It engulfs the previous candle, which shows the further direction of the market.

It is the only body candle whose open is equal to low and high is equal to close, in the case of the green candle. In the case of a red candle, open is equal to high, and close is equal to Low.

This is what engulfing candles look like.

It shows the strength of the current trend. If it is found at the bottom, it shows a bullish reversal; if it is found at the top, it shows a bearish reversal.

The psychology behind this candle is very simple. The green candle tells that buyers are ready to buy at every level, hence strong bullish momentum. The red candle tells that sellers are ready to sell at every level, hence strong bearish momentum. This candle tends to engulf the previous candle. It means if the previous candle was a red candle, and a bullish engulfing candle formed after that, this shows that bulls are ready to show strength and tend to change the direction of the market same goes with a bearish engulfing candle, if the previous candle was a green candle, and bearish engulfing candle formed, this shows that bears are ready to show the strength, and tends to change the direction of the market.

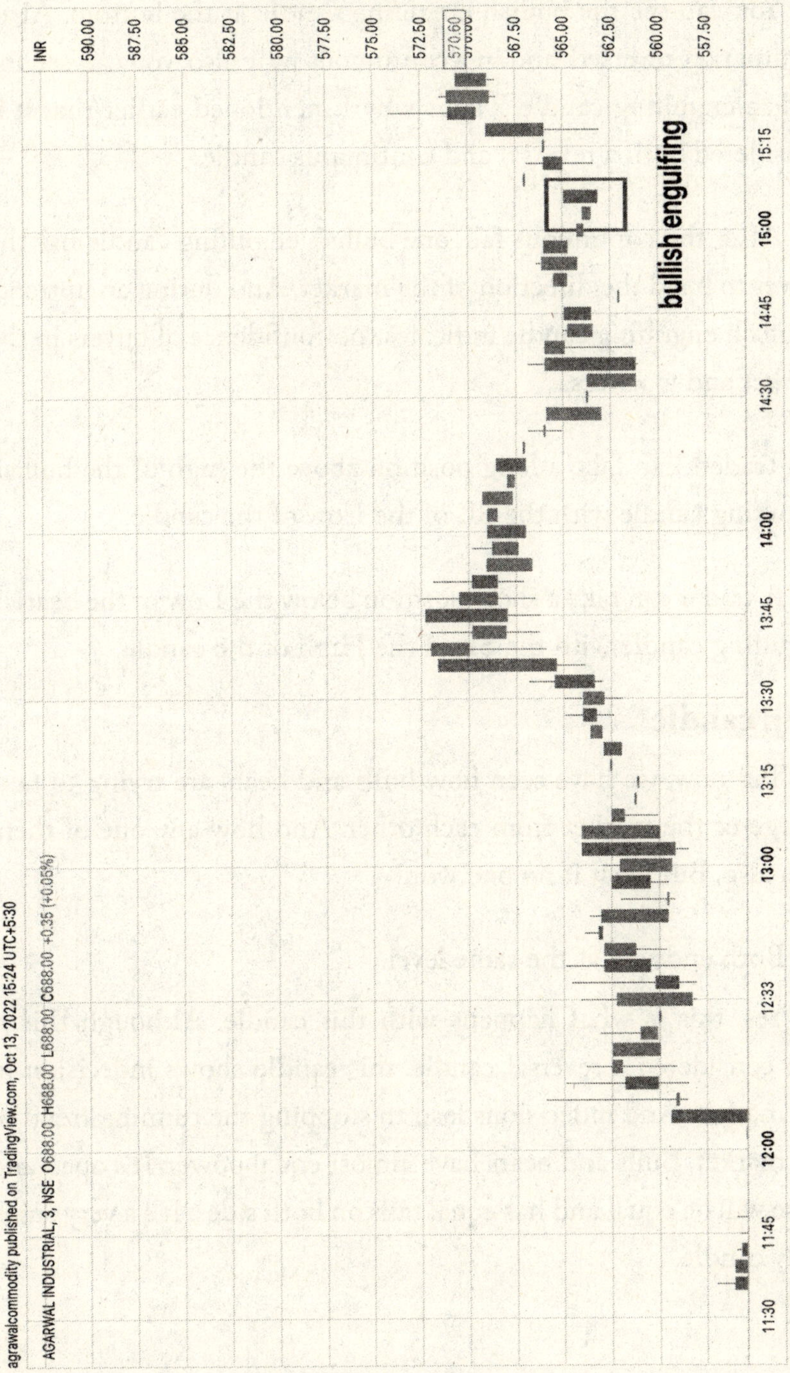
agrawalcommodity published on TradingView.com, Oct 13, 2022 15:24 UTC+5:30
AGARWAL INDUSTRIAL, 3, NSE O688.00 H688.00 L688.00 C688.00 +0.35 (+0.05%)
bullish engulfing
TradingView

You can see the bullish engulfing candle at the bottom. After that market reversed, and in a continuous rally also, you can see the bullish engulfing candle. That's why I mentioned earlier that it is considered both a reversal and continuous candle.

After the continuous fall, one bullish engulfing candle has the power to bend the direction of the market. And during an uptrend, a bullish engulfing candle indicates the confidence of buyers in the market and vice versa.

Traders can take a long position above the high of the bullish engulfing candle with the SL of the Low of the candle.

A trader can take a short position below the Low of the bearish engulfing candle with the SL of the High of the candle.

Doji candle

Till now, we have seen how bulls and bears are trying to take charge of the market from each other. And how any one of them won also. But what if no one won?

Both ends are at the same level.

Yes, this is what happens with this candle. Although this is also considered a reversal candle, this candle shows indecision in the market. And indecisions lead to stopping the running trend of the market. Bulls and bears have almost equal power. It's open and close will be equal and has equal tails on both sides. It's a very small body candle.

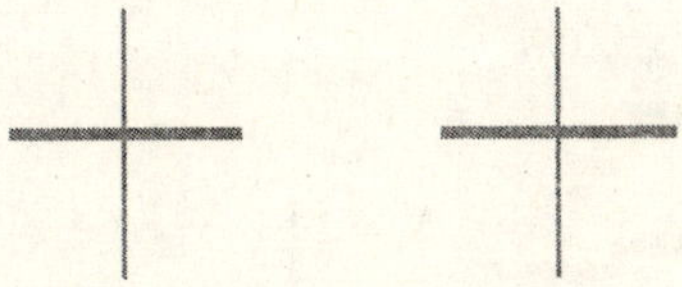

This is what a Doji candle looks like.

You will find this candle at the top or bottom anywhere. It just indicates the confusion. This means market participants are not clear with their view of where the market will move in the coming future. Buyers are not buying more, and sellers are not selling more.

Let's check-out out the chart:

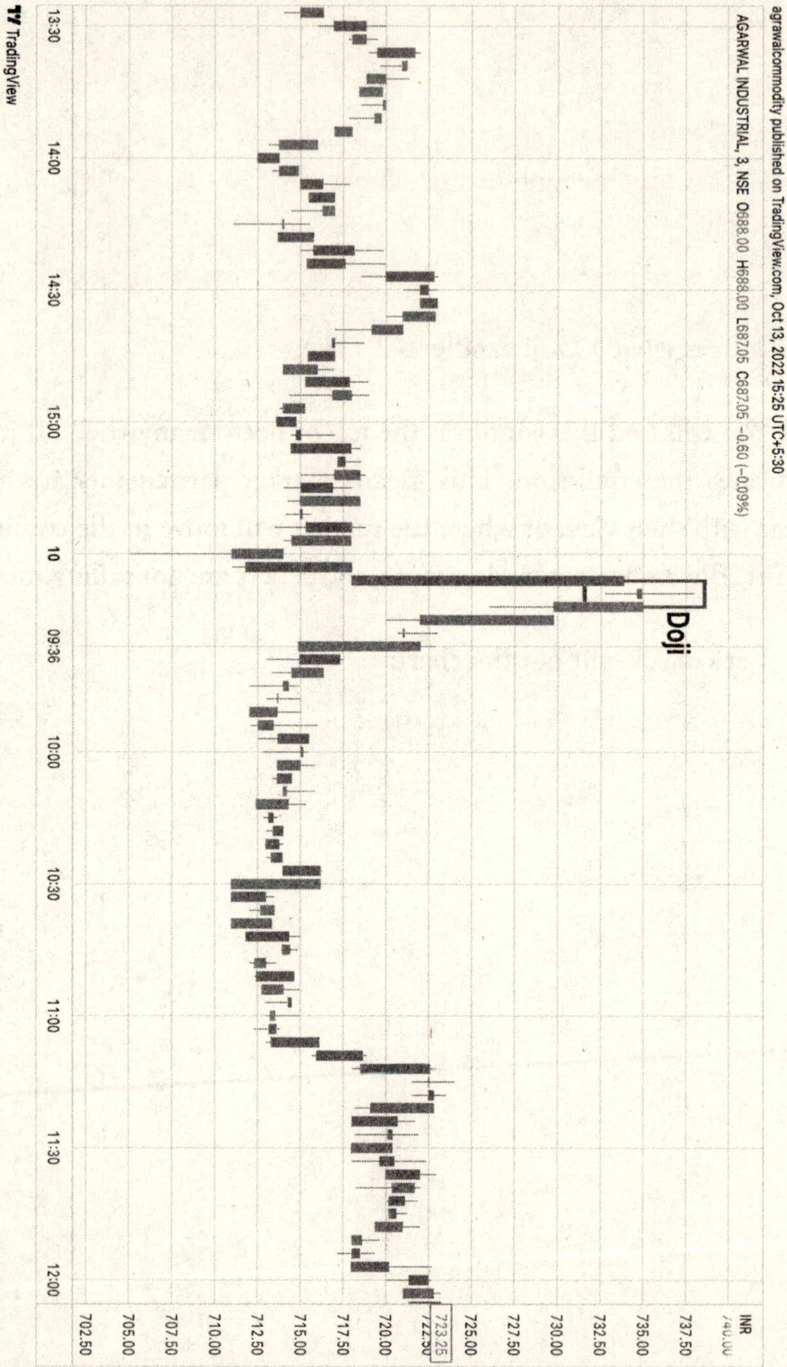
agrawalcommodity published on TradingView.com, Oct 13, 2022 15:25 UTC+5:30
AGARWAL INDUSTRIAL, 3, NSE O688.00 H688.00 L687.05 C687.05 −0.60 (−0.09%)
Doji
INR
723.25
TradingView

As you can see in the chart above, doji found at the top of the rally indicates that bulls are not comfortable in buying above this level, but at the same sellers are also not confident in selling. That's why the market closed at the same level where it started. But one thing is very clear buyers, or bulls, are now losing the confidence to buy more which may lead the previous trend to stop. We are not claiming that the market will fall from this level, but it is clear that the trend may stop. Do you need to take the confirmation from the back data if that level acted as a resistance in the past or not?

Risky traders may go short below the Low of the Doji candle, with the SL of the high of the candle.

The same goes true in the case when Doji is found at the bottom; it shows confusion, and chances of reversal are possible.

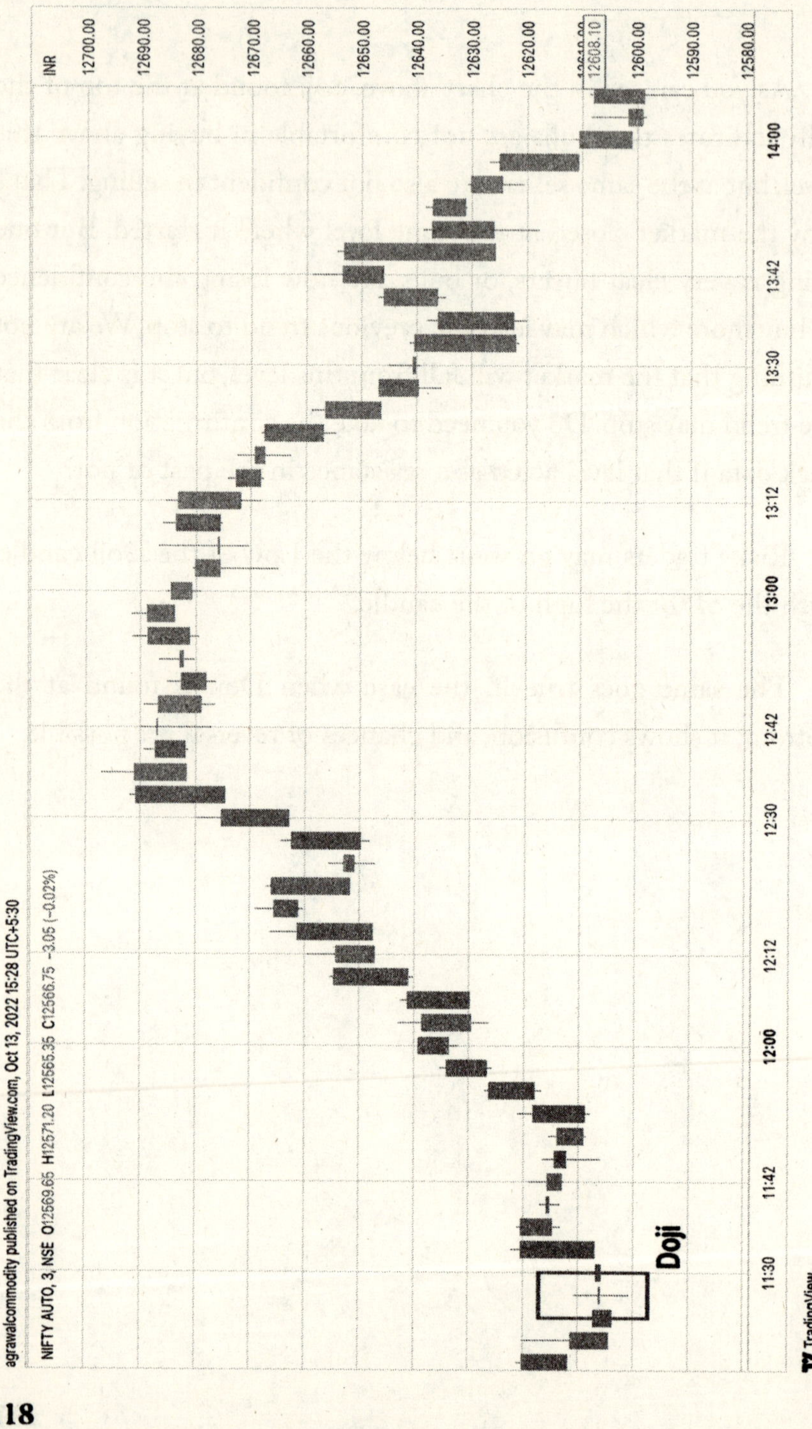
agrawalcommodity published on TradingView.com, Oct 13, 2022 15:28 UTC+5:30
NIFTY AUTO, 3, NSE O12569.65 H12571.20 L12565.35 C12566.75 -3.05 (-0.02%)
Doji
TradingView

After the continuous fall, sellers lose their confidence to sell more at the same time, and buyers are also not more confident to buy at this level.

Risky traders may go long above the high of the Doji candle, with the Sl of the Low of the candle.

So, this is all you need from candles to start your trading journey.

You must find and tag me on social media. Which candle helped you a lot? And how much money you made in that trade?

With this, we have done with the candle stick types.

As of now we have finished the basics of the technical analysis. Now we will start with the Advance concept of technical analysis.

MOMENTUM

Let's create a situation where we have to check the knowledge strength of two students.

How we can do that?

We need to check the rate of change of the marks of the students across different subjects.

For understanding, rate of change is defined as how fast something moves.

So, in order to know the knowledge strength of the students, we need to have marks of two students at least so, that we can compare the strength by analyzing the rate of change.

Assume, we have two students: A & B

Marks of both students are:

	E	H	M	S	S	Total
A	0	5	10	15	20	10
B	0	10	20	30	40	20

Let's draw a chart of the marks, which gives you a visual representation of the marks and the rate of change.

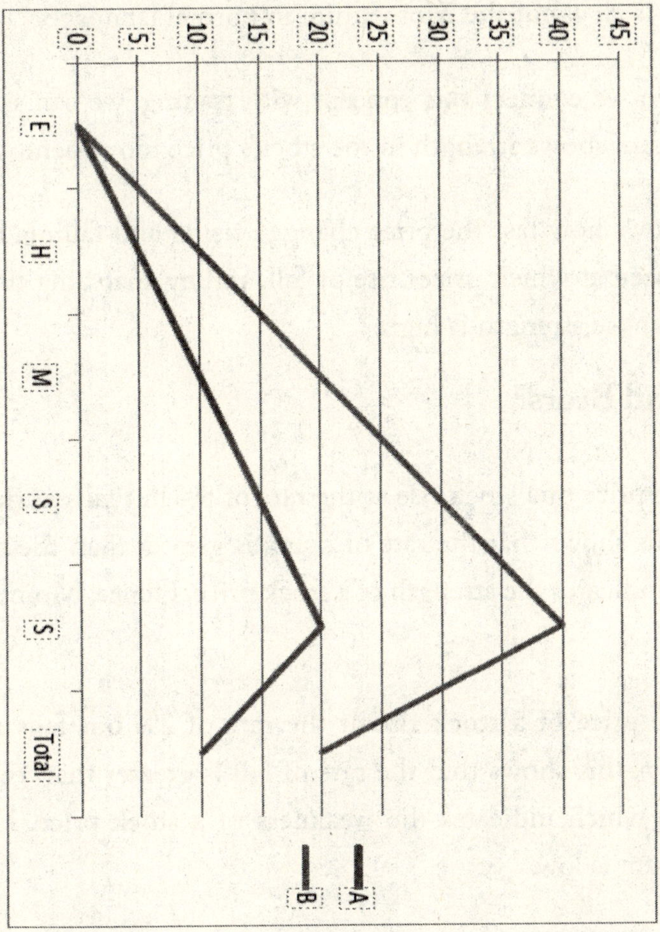

As you can see, it is very clear that B's rate of change in marks is high.

What does it mean? If you see the marks table, A's rate of change of marks is 5, and B's rate of change of marks is ten across the subjects.

It clearly shows that B's rate of change of marks is higher than A's. This means B's knowledge strength is high as compared to A's.

This is all about the Momentum in normal language.

When we connect this concept with trading, we can say that Momentum shows strength in the stock's price movement.

It shows how fast the price changes, rising and falling. It tells us the speed at which prices rise or fall, and by analyzing that, we can say whose strength is high.

Bulls and Bears?

If the price of a stock rise at the rate of 5% but falls at the rate of 2%, this shows that the rate of rising is greater than the rate of fall; this indicates the strength of a stock price. Hence, Momentum is high.

If the price of a stock rise at the rate of 2% but falls at the rate of 5%, this shows that the rate of fall is greater than the rate of rising, which indicates the weakness of a stock price. Hence, Momentum is low.

Investors/ Traders use the Momentum to confirm the strength of the trend. It generally works wonderfully in a rising market compared to a falling market.

How do we measure Momentum?

We are going quite statistical. Right? Don't worry; you don't have to do any calculations. We will deal with the indicators which indicate the Momentum of the stock's price. You will get all these indicators in any technical charting software.

The rate of change in momentum is what momentum indicators gauge.

Price is changing as opposed to actual price change. Similar kind while calculating a stock's momentum. If the rate of increase is what we're looking for, fall is either keeping a certain amount of force or losing it as the price.

RSI (Relative Strength Indicator)

I have already given you a glimpse of RSI in the indicators section. As indicated in the name of this indicator itself. It shows the relative strength of the price.

As I said earlier, RSI moves in a range of 0 – 100. As per the traditional theory, if RSI is above 70, it is considered an overbought situation. If RSI is below 30, it is considered an oversold situation.

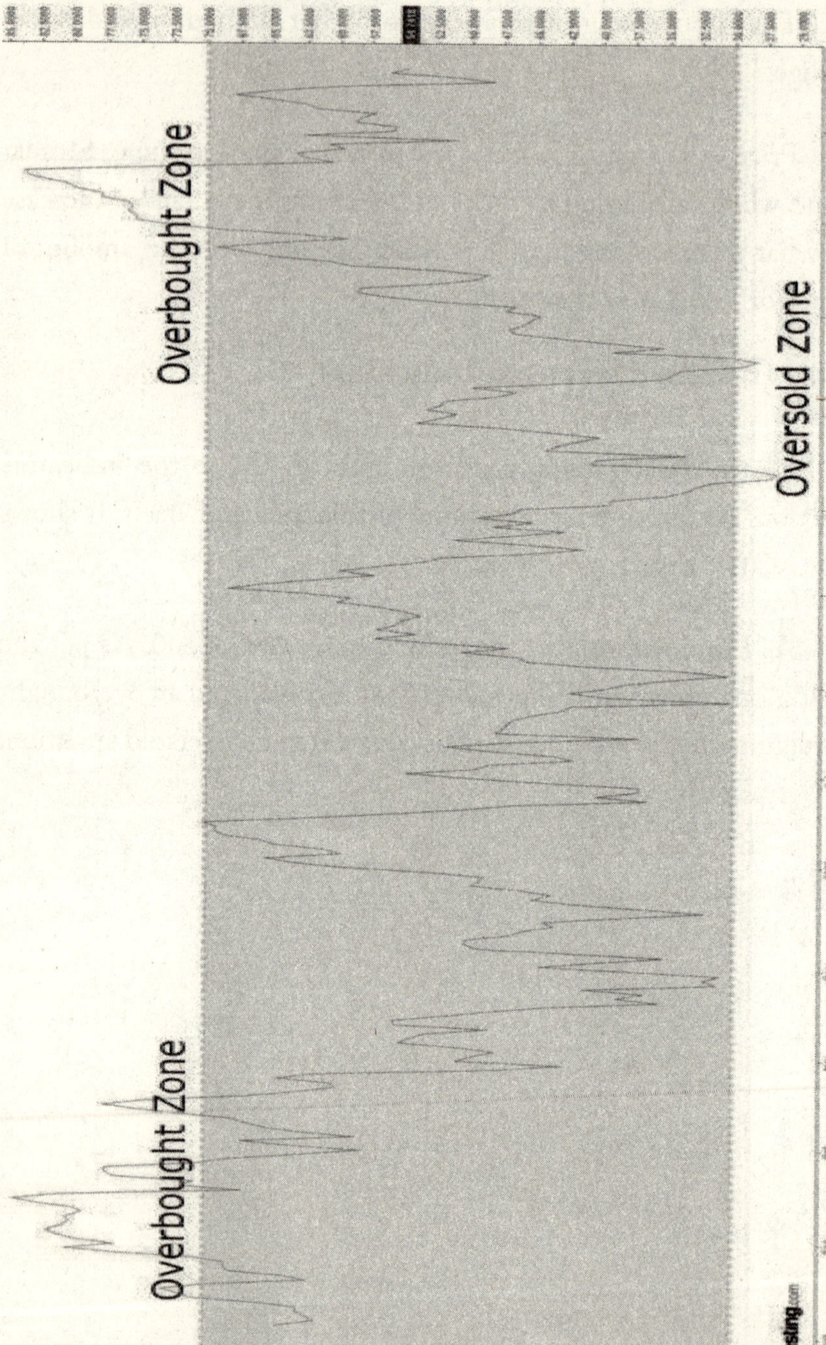
Overbought Zone
Oversold Zone
Overbought Zone
Investing.com

As RSI is rising, it shows the upcoming strength in the stock price, which may lead to a big move in the stock price.

If RSI is falling, it shows the upcoming weakness in the stock price, which may lead to a big fall in the stock price.

RSI acts as a confirmation tool in trading set-ups.

Modern theories suggest that you can predict the future Momentum in the stock through RSI.

If RSI crosses above 60, this indicates that Momentum is the stock price about to come in the upside direction.

Likewise, if it crosses below 40, this indicates that the stock price is losing Momentum and may fall heavily.

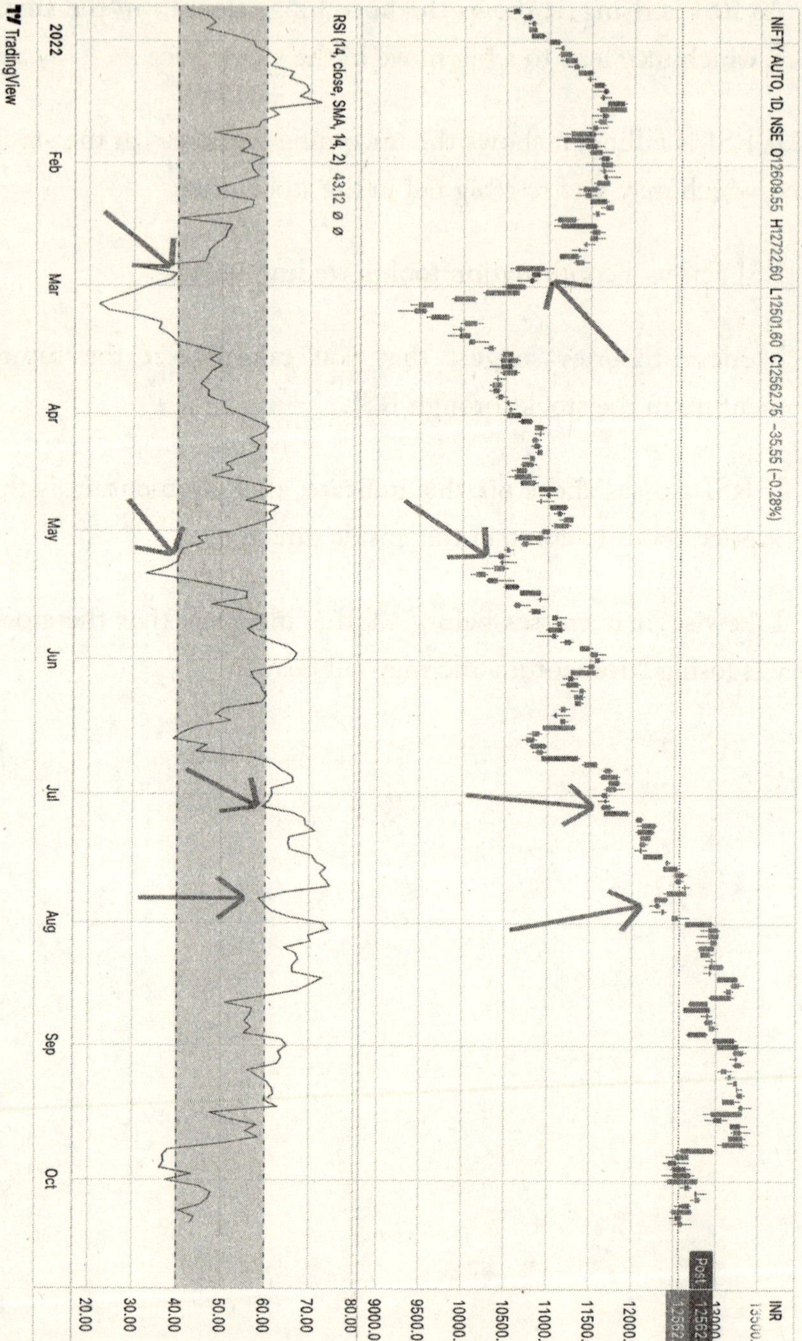
agrawalcommodity published on TradingView.com, Oct 13, 2022 15:32 UTC+5:30
NIFTY AUTO, 1D, NSE O12609.55 H12722.60 L12501.60 C12562.75 -35.55 (-0.28%)
RSI (14, close, SMA, 14, 2) 43.12 ø ø
2022
Feb
Mar
Apr
May
Jun
Jul
Aug
Sep
Oct
INR
TradingView

RSI Divergence is also one of the trading set-ups in the trading universe and is often used by traders.

RSI divergence means RSI is moving against the direction of the price, which indicates the current trend's weakness and the possible reversal.

If the stock price is rising and RSI is falling, this indicates the weakness in the price, and it may fall anytime. Therefore, trades should exit from their long positions and may trail Stop loss.

If the stock price is falling and RSI is rising, this again indicates the weakness in the current trend, which may reverse anytime. Therefore, trades should exit from their short positions and may trail Stop loss.

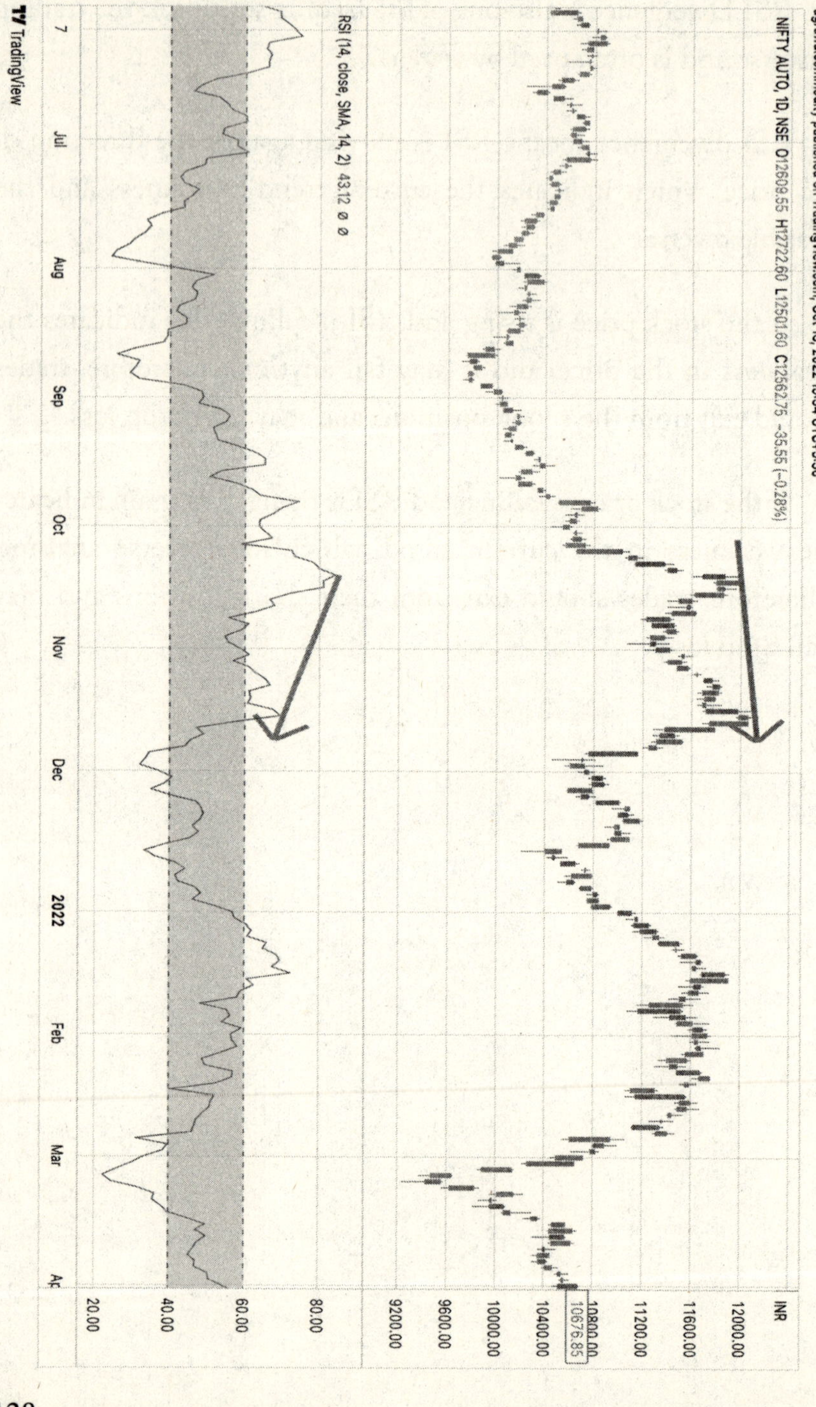
agrawalcommodity published on TradingView.com, Oct 13, 2022 15:34 UTC+5:30
NIFTY AUTO, 1D, NSE O12609.55 H12722.60 L12501.60 C12562.75 −35.55 (−0.28%)
RSI (14, close, SMA, 14, 2) 43.12 ø ø
TradingView

See the divergence in RSI and price. Price is making higher high, but RSI is making lower high. This divergence is the indication of the reversal. It indicates that the price may fall from this point, and as you can see price fall from that point. This is what we call a prediction of the future move of the price.

Another Indicator that helps you to catch the Momentum of the stock market is MACD.

MACD

I have already discussed the basics of MACD in the indicator section, and here we will see the application part.

How can you use the MACD to analyze the market moves? We all know that MACD shows the relation between two EMA, 24 EMA, and 12 EMA; this gives the use of a MACD line.

One more line in the MACD is a signal line, which is nothing but the 9 EMA. We can use any time frame, minute, hours, day, week, or month- MACD will shift accordingly. When the MACD line crosses above the signal line, it indicates bullish Momentum. Hence, trigger buying signal. When the MACD line crosses below the signal line, it indicates bearish Momentum. Hence, trigger a selling signal.

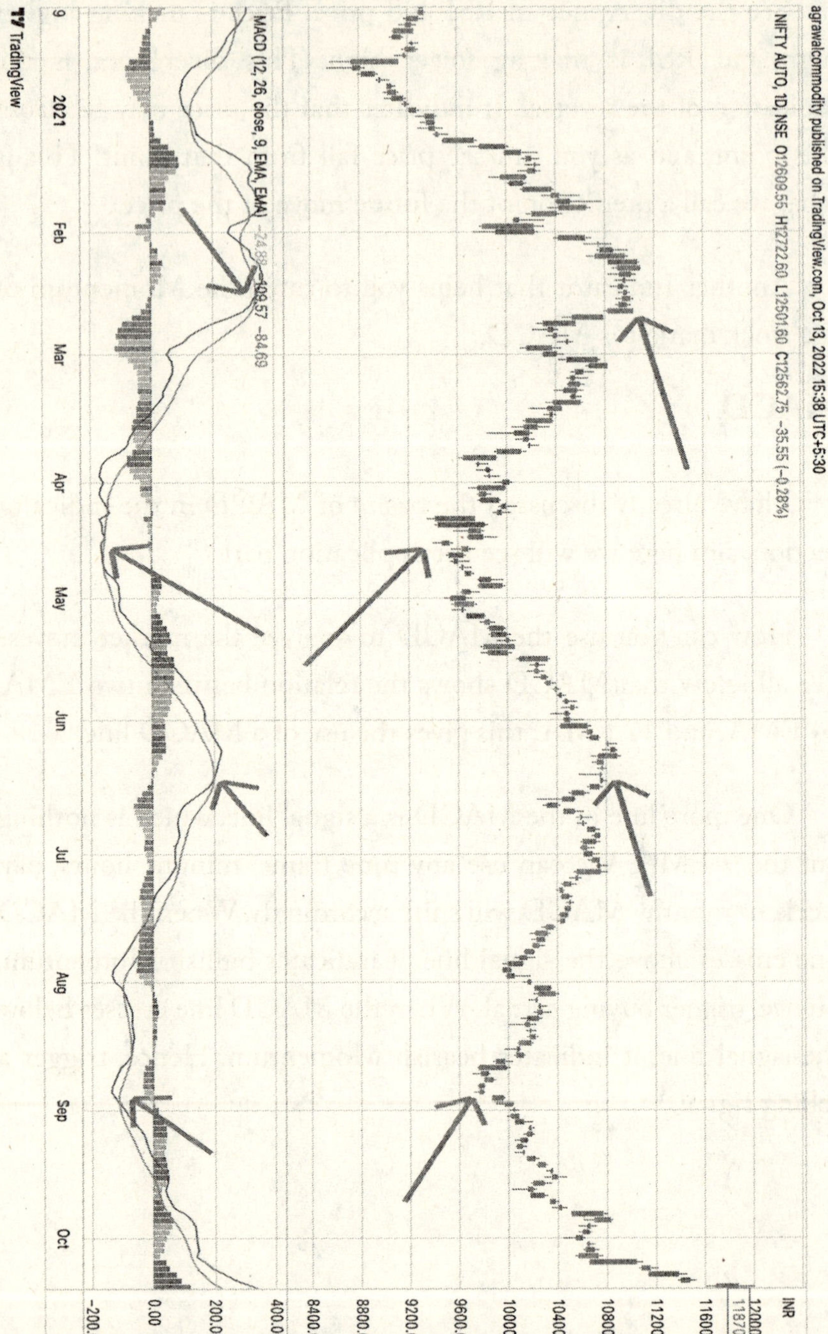
agrawalcommodity published on TradingView.com, Oct 13, 2022 15:38 UTC+5:30
NIFTY AUTO, 1D, NSE O12609.55 H12722.60 L12501.60 C12562.75 −35.55 (−0.28%)
INR
MACD (12, 26, close, 9, EMA, EMA) −24.88 −109.57 −84.69
TradingView
9
2021
Feb
Mar
Apr
May
Jun
Jul
Aug
Sep
Oct
12000.00
11870.00
11600.00
11200.00
10800.00
10400.00
10000.00
9600.00
9200.00
8800.00
8400.00
400.00
200.00
0.00
-200.00

See how MACD works; it indicates the upcoming Momentum in the stock price. You can use both RSI and MACD as a trading set-up to execute the trade.

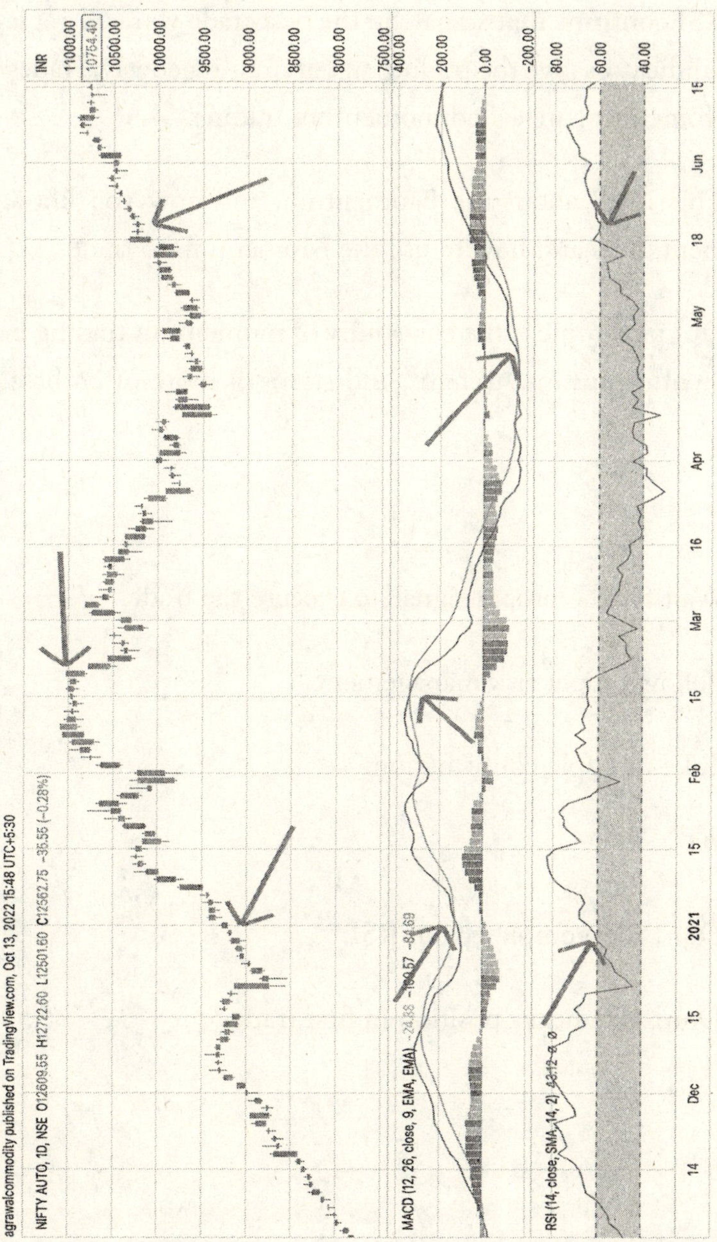

As you can see in the chart above, both the indicators givc the trading signal, but if you observe that MACD has given a signal before RSI, it means that MACD first triggers the trading signal, but RSI confirms that signal. So the best trade you will get is when both indicators give the trading signal simultaneously. Trades based on Momentum are called momentum trading.

This is all about the Momentum, and now you know what Momentum is and how to use the Momentum to trade.

Our next topic is the continuity of momentum trading because Momentum means strength, and strength more often breaks the levels.

Do's

Wait for the proper signal, to execute the trade.

Follow proper risk management

Take multiple confirmations

Don't

Don't rely completely on RSI.

Don't take heavy position in first trade.

Breakout & Breakdown

This is one of the crucial topics you need to understand for momentum trading. Remember we discussed the support and resistance in the previous chapter?

Let's brush up on the concept once:

Support is the point at which buyers are more active, and sellers are unwilling to sell below the support point. In stocks, a support price may act as the right price to buy per the buyers. This leads to a rise in the price of the stock when it hits the support price.

Resistance is when sellers are more active, and buyers are unwilling to buy above the resistance point. In stocks, the resistance price may act as an overpriced zone to sell the stock as per the sellers. This leads to a fall in share price when it hits the resistance price.

Breakout & Breakdown

Two most important and easy topics.

I hope you remember the lines I mentioned in the support and resistance section. What if the price moves above resistance? This might signal that the price may move aggressively on the upside, and similarly, if the price moves below the support point, this might be a signal that the price may fall aggressively.

That movement above and below is called Breakout and Breakdown. When the price breaks above the resistance point, it is called a Breakout.

When the price breaks below the resistance point, it is called a Breakdown. Yes, it is that simple.

As we know, it is quite difficult to break the support and resistance point, because that point reflects the power of the majority; that's why it becomes support and resistance.

So, which means that if somehow these points break, something is happening behind the scene that we as retail traders don't know, but big traders may know; that's why they bought above the resistance and below support. So this is the psychology behind the breakout and breakdown.

This activity indicates that the market may move in a breakout and breakdown direction because the majority of traders/ investors are involved in the breakout & breakdown.

The breakout indicates that the market may move on the upside.

The breakdown indicates that the market may move to the downside.

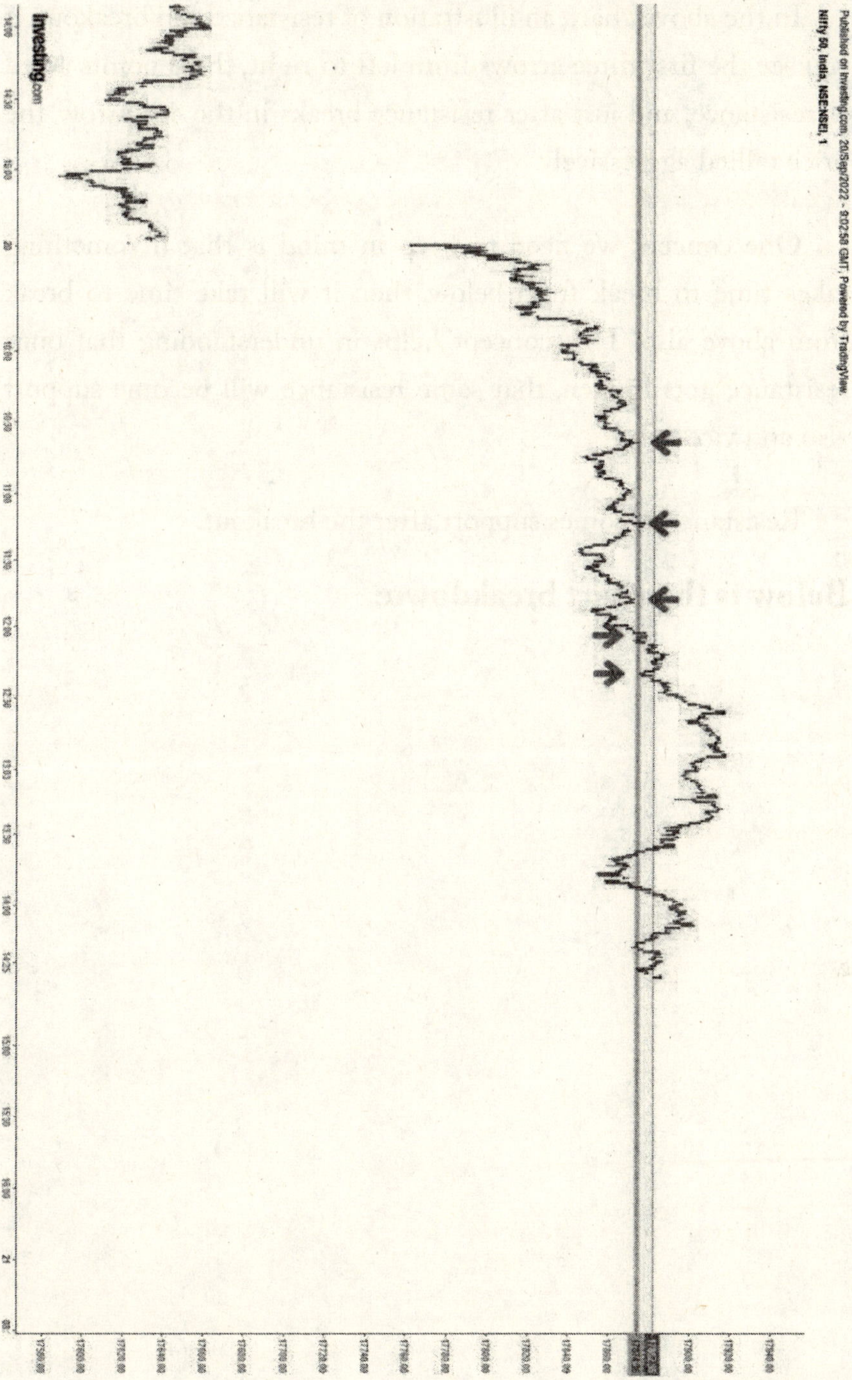
Published on Investing.com, 20/Sep/2022 - 9:02:58 GMT, Powered by TradingView.
Nifty 50, India, NSE:NSEI, 1
Investing.com

In the above chart, an illustration of resistance and breakout, if you see the first three arrows from left to right, these points acted as resistance, and just after resistance breaks in the 4th arrow, the price rallied aggressively.

One concept we need to keep in mind is that if something takes time to break from below, then it will take time to break from above also. This concept helps in understanding that once resistance gets broken, that same resistance will become support also and vice-versa.

Resistance becomes support after the breakout.

Below is the chart breakdown:

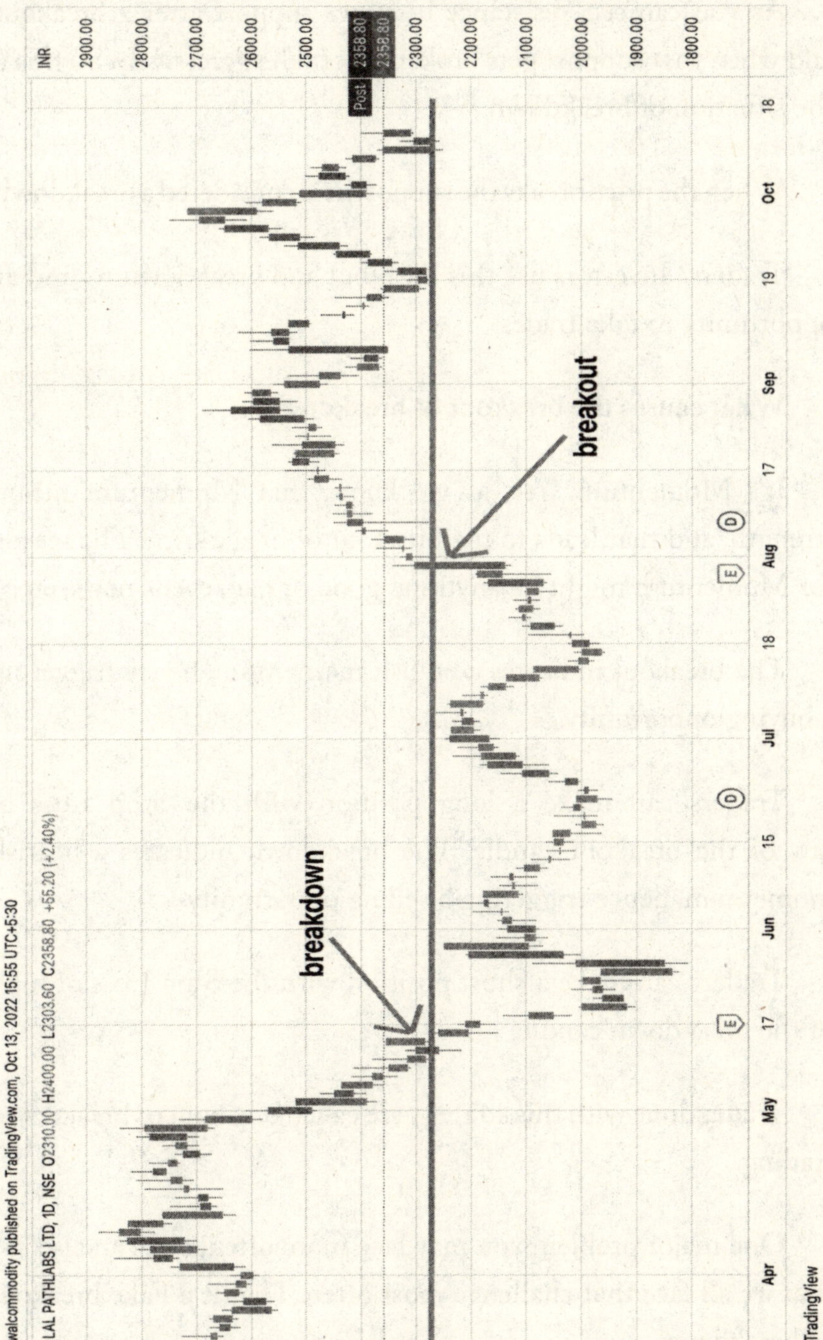
agrawalcommodity published on TradingView.com, Oct 13, 2022 15:55 UTC+5:30
DR LAL PATHLABS LTD, 1D, NSE O2310.00 H2400.00 L2303.60 C2358.80 +55.20 (+2.40%)
breakdown
breakout
TradingView

As you can see, resistance becomes support after a breakout, and when that support gets broken price fall aggressively. So this is the situation of breakdown.

When the price breaks the support, it is considered a breakdown.

Traders/ Investors use this breakout and breakdown to find an opportunity to take trades.

What causes the breakout & breakdown?

It's Momentum. Yes, as we know, that Momentum means strength, and that leads to the breakout or breakdown. The reason for Momentum might be anything good or bad, even/ news, etc.

The breakout indicates a bullish momentum, hence triggering a buying opportunity.

Traders can make a long position with the Stop Loss of low of the breakout candle. The breakdown indicates a bearish momentum, hence triggering a selling opportunity.

Traders can make a short position with the Stop Loss of high of the breakdown candle.

Trades done with this strategy are called breakout or breakdown trading.

One major problem you may face more often, or I can also say that we all face that challenge most often. That is a Fake breakout or breakdown.

As per the basic concept, we all know that after breakout and breakdown, prices tend to move in the direction of breakout and breakdown.

But you can find that breakout or breakdown is fake. After the breakout also, the price comes back below the resistance point, and after the breakdown, the price comes back above the support point.

So, fake breakout or breakdown is the main issue of this strategy. Every problem has a solution also.

The solution to this fake breakout and breakdown problem is Volume analysis, which is also our next topic.

Volume

Theoretically, I cannot change the definition of volume, i.e., a total number of shares traded is called volume. But I'll clear your concept in the best possible way. Let's understand with an example: You bought and sold 1000 shares. It means you bought 1000 and sold 1000, a total of 2000 shares traded. This is called volume.

You can also call this a total turnover of shares.

Volumes won't tell you anything alone. This means if you can only see volume, you won't be able to analyze much about the market and future moves.

It works wonderfully when combined with other tools.

Do you remember the problem we were facing in breakout & breakdown trading? Fake breakout and breakdown problem.

Volumes play a vital role in solving that problem, and it gives us confirmation of if the breakout is real or fake.

When I use the term "volume," I'm referring to the overall number of shares traded in a stock or market within a specific time frame.

Volume can be monitored for practically any time period, including daily, weekly, monthly, etc.

Let's understand how?

Until now, we know that a breakout means the price moves above the resistance, and Momentum leads that breakout; it clearly means that most market participants are willing to buy above the the resistance point. So, we can also say that if the majority really wants to buy above resistance, then it should have the volume above resistance or at breakout candle. The same is true in case of breakdown also. Sometimes what happens is like a few players start placing buying orders above the resistance point, which leads to the breakout, but because of the lack of the majority of participants, the price is not able to sustain above the resistance point. It also means that few people with lots of money can operate the market. Yes, that's true. That's the reason we need to track the volume and also to get confirmation of the price move. The volume makes the shares more liquid, and it is difficult to operate liquid shares. That reduces the chance of fake breakouts or breakdowns.

After volume confirmation, you will get 60-70% successful breakout or breakdown trading. Why not 100%? This is because this market runs by humans and human- made machines; the possibility of uncertainty is always there in the market.

You will find the volume on any technical chart.

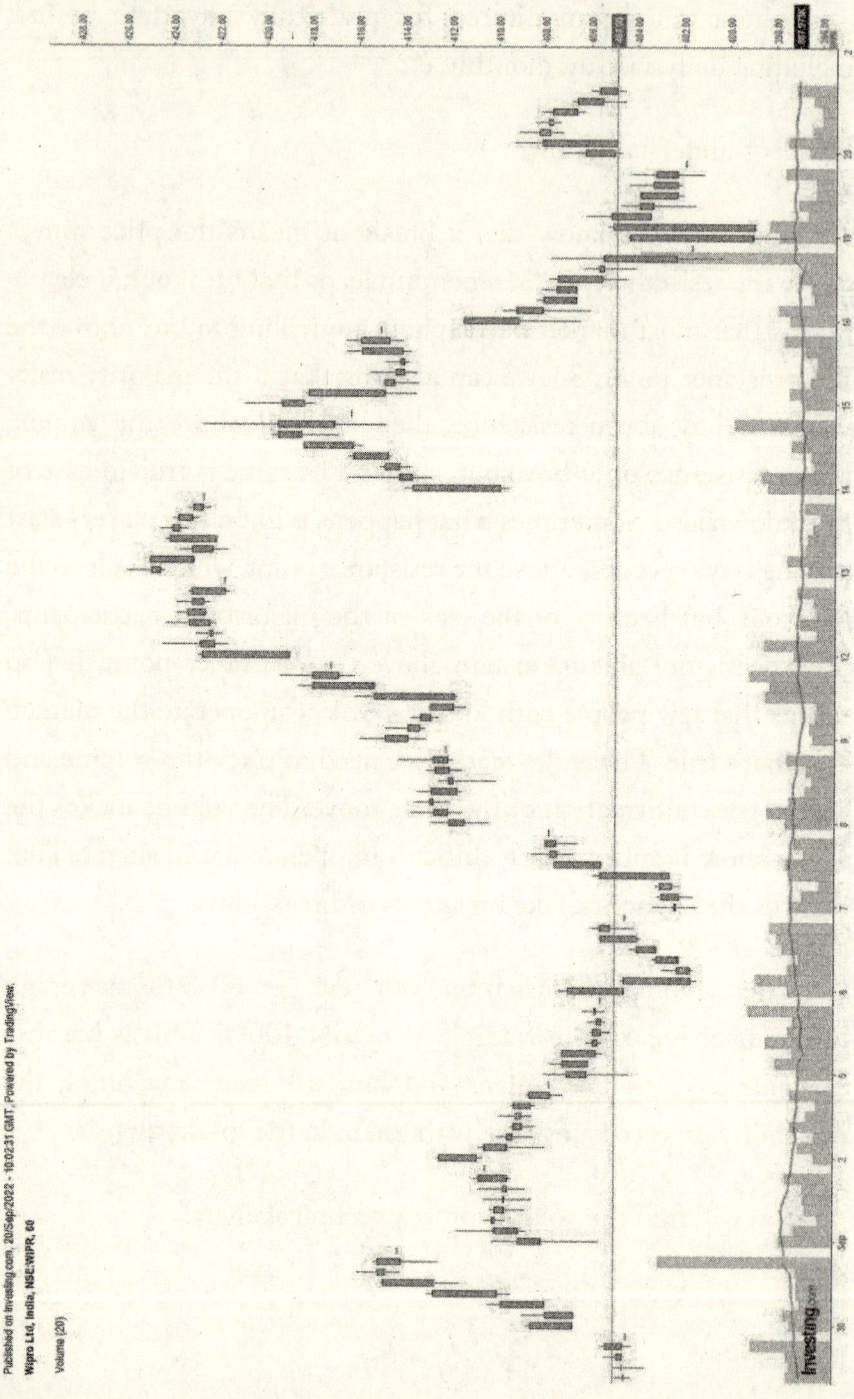
Published on Investing.com, 20/Sep/2022 - 10:02:31 GMT, Powered by TradingView.
Wipro Ltd, India, NSE:WIPR, 60
Volume (20)
Investing.com

The bar below the candle stick chart is a volume chart.

It shows green in case of buying and red in case of selling.

An essential component of your technical education should be the volume study and its relation to price action. It is the second most researched piece of information that analysts will employ, after price, for reasons that will become evident. Price is the most important information in technical analysis, but volume is the best overall indicator of an investor's involvement in price movement. The technician's confirmation tool, this data point is used in practically every aspect of our work.

Other types of technical analysis use volume in different ways to identify trends, validate price movement, and determine where the money is moving.

A Decline In Volume

Generally speaking, through out long periods of decline, total

Volume tends to drop significantly. Investors typically hold off on making new purchases during bear markets, which results in decreased volume and reduced entire portfolios. Typically, a prolonged decline's final days

Watch volume rise, but investors finally give up, it is viewed as a sign of capitulation. Many investors may exit the stock market during a bear market and move their money to safer investments like money market funds or the bond market.

Fibonacci

You must have studied the 3 Laws of Newton in your schools. Relax; I am not going to discuss that.

I just want to connect you with the point that a few things we need to accept as introduced.

Like, we can't question Newton's law. Right?

So, from this I want you to introduce one of the universal concepts known as Fibonacci.

It's a number sequence, Developed by Italy-based mathematician "Leonardo Fibonacci" in the late 13th century.

I don't want to indulge in the core concepts of Fibonacci.

I'll go straight to the topic, which helps you make money by trading. Fibonacci has given us three numbers, which are called the Golden Numbers.

These golden numbers help the trader to find support and resistance. And just for the information, I want to tell you that everything around you follows the Fibonacci sequence.

Those golden numbers are:

.382, .50, .618

These levels work wonderfully in trading by acting as support and resistance. When the market is in the bull phase, and you missed the rally, you must wait for a 2nd chance to enter and enjoy the rally.

You know that market won't move in a straight line, recall the trend concept. Price moves in a zig-zag pattern.

So, it means the market must correct itself or you can also say that market must fall after a certain level of a rally.

To find the level up to which the market may fall and bounce back to continue the rally, we can use Fibonacci levels.

Remember this point will give you 2nd chance to enter the rally.

According to the traders and what is observed from the past analysis, when the market is in an uptrend and just after 1st straight rally when the market starts correcting, it may hit the maximum of three levels to bounce back and continue the rally.

1st level is .382 or 38.2%; this will be the 1st support when the price corrects from the top.

2nd level is .50 or 50%, this will be the 2nd support when the price corrects from the top, and it is obvious that to touch this level, the price should break .382.

3rd level is .618 or 61.8%, this will be the 3rd and most important support when the price corrects from the top. If the price breaks below this level, this might be an indication of the trend change.

The same condition you will find in case of a downtrend also.

When the market is in a downtrend, and just after 1st straight fall, when the market starts an upside pull back, it may hit the maximum of 3 levels to bounce back and continue the fall.

1st level is .382 or 38.2%, this will be the 1st resistance when the price rises from the bottom.

2nd level is .50 or 50%, this will be the 2nd resistance when the price rises from the bottom, and it is obvious that to touch this level, the price should break .382. 3rd level is .618 or 61.8%, this will be the 3rd and most important resistance when the price rises from the bottom. If the Price breaks above this level, this might be an indication of the trend change.

Now let's see how Fibonacci looks and how to draw.

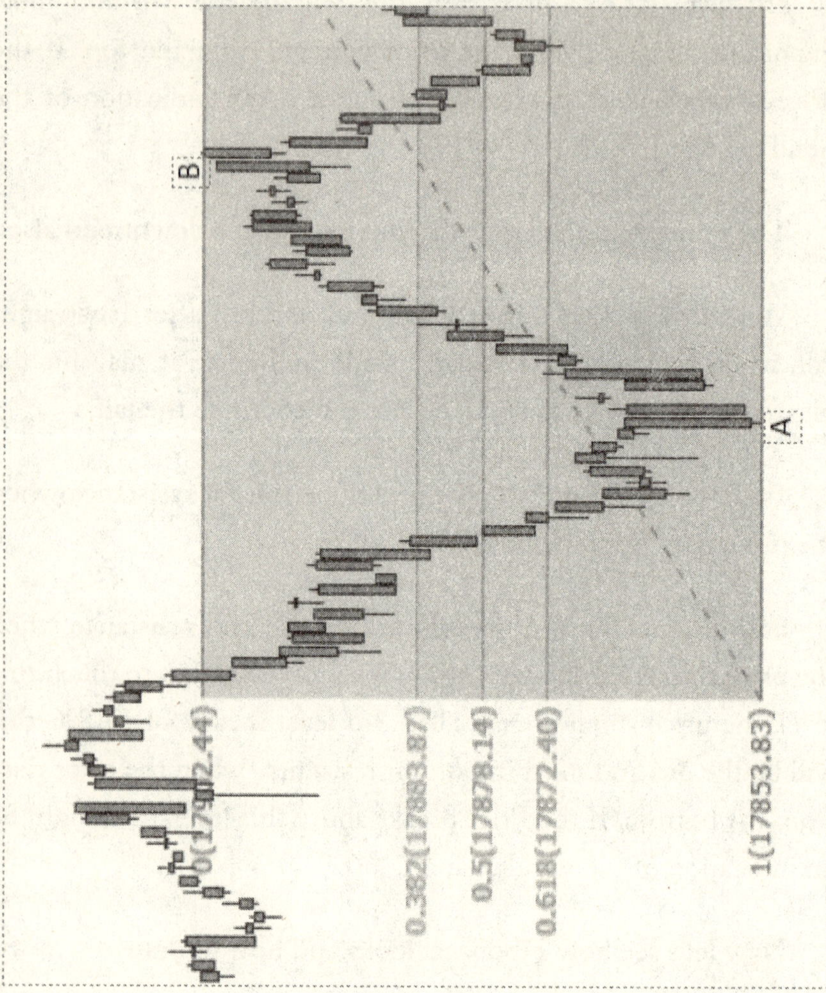

As you can see in the figure above, the market price rallied from point A to point

B. And starts correcting from point B, try to notice that the market also tried to stop at the 0.382 level of Fibonacci. But unable to hold that level and falls further, but at 0.618, markets held and bounced back to continue the rally.

In Bull Run, in order to find a support point, you need to draw a Fibonacci from the recent swing low to the recent swing high.

Let's see the Fibonacci levels acting as a resistance.

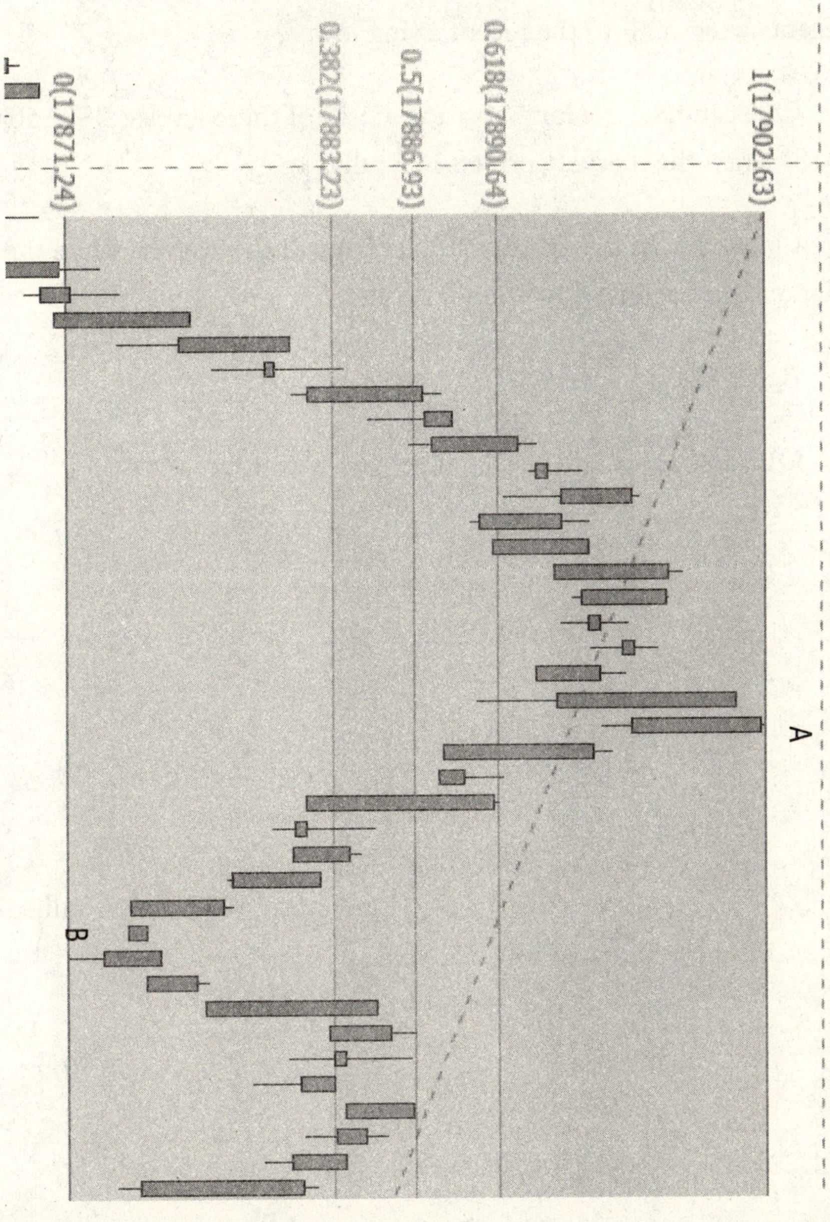

As you can see in the figure above, the market price falls from point A to point B. And starts correcting from point B, but at 0.50 market hold and continues the fall. In a Bearish market, in order to find a resistance point, you need to draw a Fibonacci from the recent swing high to the recent swing low.

One can take the long position at any of these levels (.382, .50, .618) when the market corrects in a rally.

One can take the short position at any of these levels when the market corrects in a downtrend.

Relax, not finished yet.

Our next topic will also connect you with Fibonacci.

Fibonacci Extensions

Where is support if a price drops to a new low that has never been reached before? By definition, there cannot be support based on prior price activity when a price hits a new record low. Similar to this, based on prior price movement, there must be overhead resistance when a price sets a new record high.

How are Fibonacci extensions made? The most important number for our analysis is a number in the Fibonacci sequence can be divided by the number before it to get the number 1.618. As an illustration, 89 x 55 Equals 1.618, or 161.8%. 1.618 has a square root of 1.272 (127.2%). Furthermore, Fibonacci extensions typically use that number.

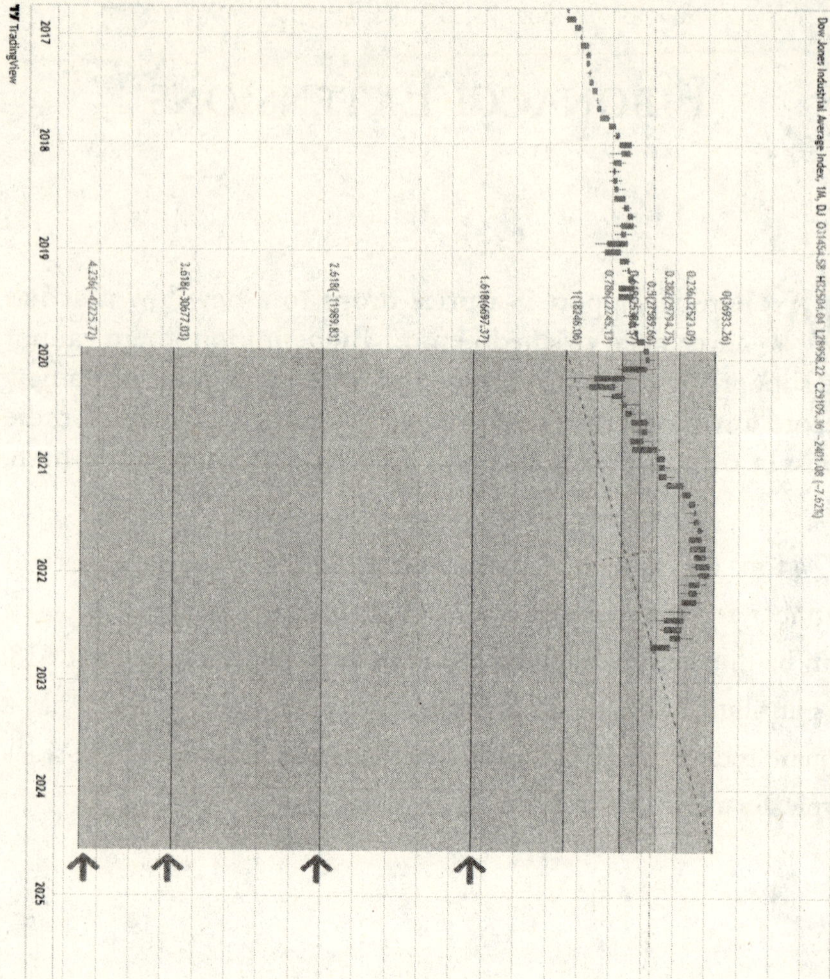
agrawalcontent published on TradingView.com, Sep 29, 2022 19:43 UTC-5:30
Dow Jones Industrial Average Index, 1M, DJ O31454.58 H32504.04 L28958.22 C31105.36 −2401.08 (−7.62%)
0(36933.26)
0.236(32523.09)
0.382(29794.75)
0.5(27589.66)
0.786(22245.13)
1(18246.06)
1.618(6697.37)
2.618(−11989.83)
3.618(−30677.03)
4.236(−42225.72)
TradingView

This is what Extension Looks like in downside.

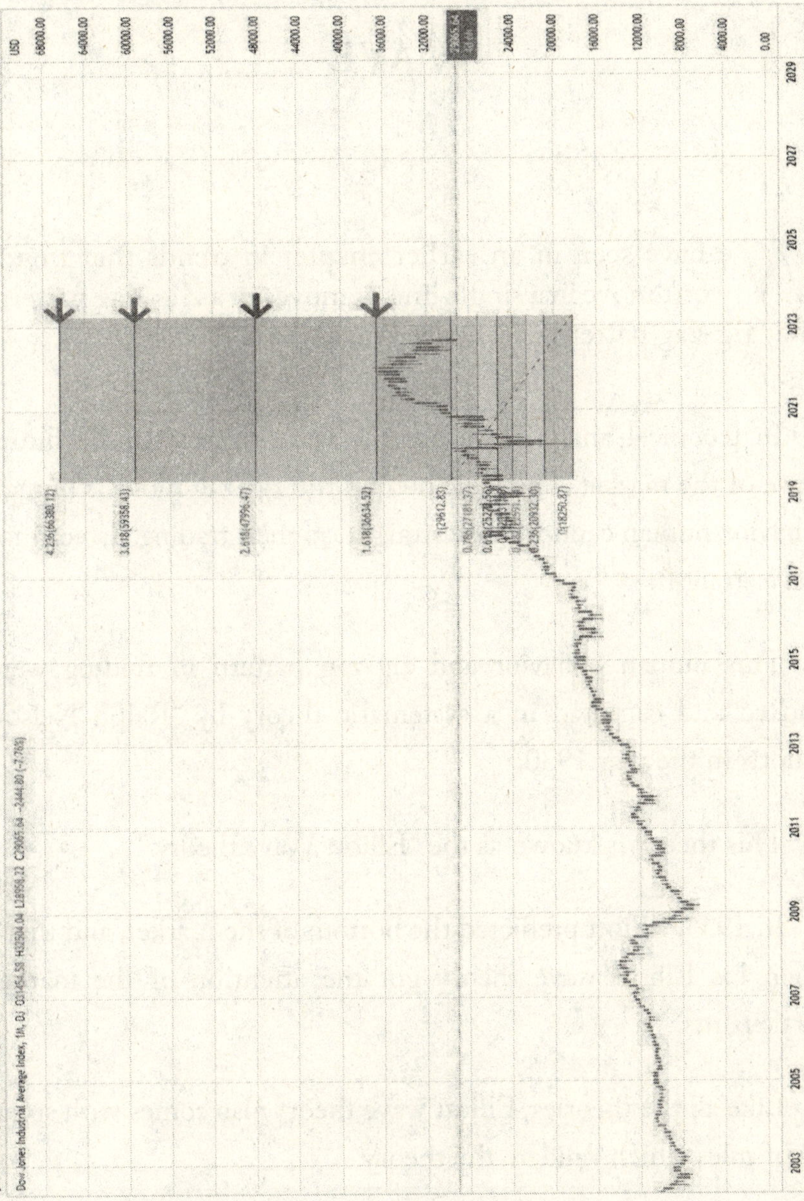

In order to identify new high from all time high, you can use the extension level, which will give you the new resistance level.

Wave

We have seen in an earlier chapter in trends that trends won't move in a single line. It moves in a Zig Zag pattern. That zig-zag pattern is called a Wave.

In technical analysis, we use the wave to predict the future move of the market. The logic behind the zig-zag move is human behavior, human cannot move straight, so their trading also cannot move straight.

This human behavior and zig-zag pattern in trading were tracked and captured in a systematic theory by "Ralph Nelson Elliott" in the year 1930.

This theory is known as the "Elliott Wave theory."

In 1935, Elliott predicted the bottom of the market, and that's when his Elliott wave theory got the attention of the market participants.

Like all the theories, Elliott wave theory also comes with some set of rules which validate the theory.

As per the beliefs of this theory, that zig-zag pattern of the price which they call a wave is created by the psychology of the market participants.

This theory defines the wave in two types:

1st is Impulsive Waves

2nd is Corrective Waves

Let's recall the primary trend of the Dow Theory, the longest trend, which lasts over 1 or 2 years.

According to Elliott Wave theory, this is an impulsive wave; under which 5 sub- waves are also available. Those 5 sub-waves together move in the same direction as the primary trend.

It means five sub-waves will make one impulsive wave, which will be the major trend.

It has some set of rules; without these rules, the impulsive wave will be invalid.

1st. The second wave should not correct more than 100% of the first wave

2nd. The third wave should never be the shortest of 1st 3rd and 5th waves.

3rd. The fourth wave should never overlap 1st wave.

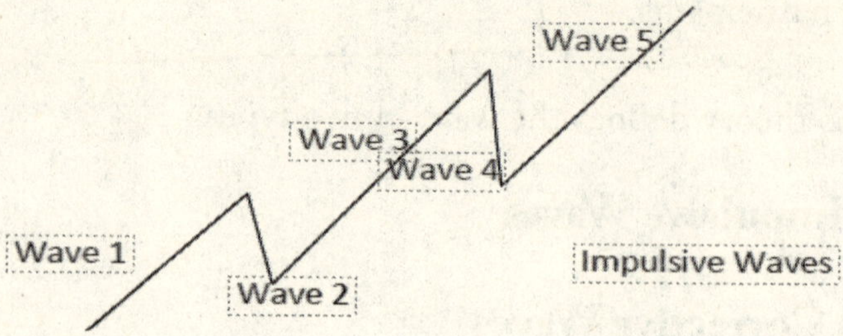

This is what impulsive waves look like when you follow the rules of the theory. To know the level up to which wave two might fall, you can use Fibonacci levels. Now we have corrective waves. Which also is the combination of 3 sub-waves?

Like in impulsive waves, sub-waves move in the direction of the main trend of an impulsive wave.

In corrective waves also, its sub-waves move in the direction of corrective waves. Corrective waves move in the opposite direction of impulsive wave.

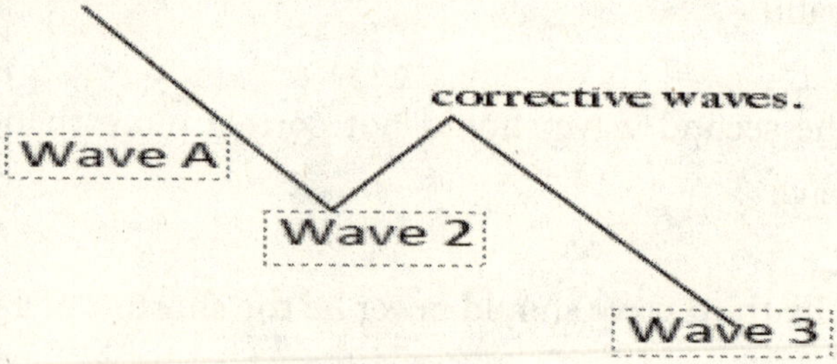

This is how Corrective waves look. You can relate this to the secondary trend of the Dow Theory.

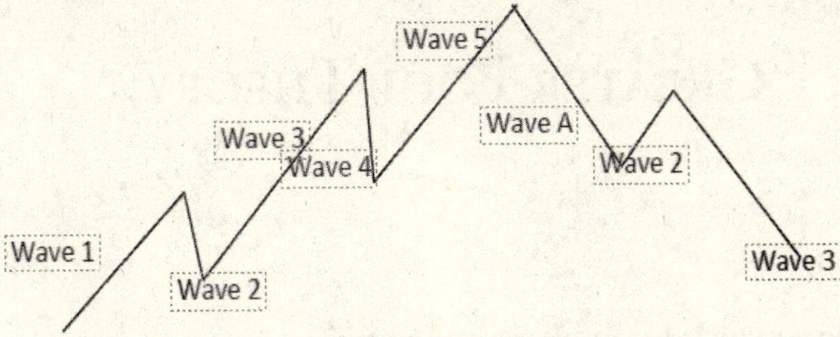

This is what you will get when you combine impulsive and corrective waves.

By analyzing the waves, traders can predict the future move of the market. To get the levels of the corrective wave, we can use Fibonacci levels.

Every impulsive wave consists of five sub-waves, and the pattern continues. The next theory which I am going to discuss is a very interesting theory; we are using this theory in day-to-day life also, but we never notice it.

Greater Fool Theory

Do you ever have such a situation??

When you bought a second-hand product at a higher price, but you found that it won't deserve to be paid that much.

And you sold that product to someone else even at a higher price or at least at the same price you bought.

What did you do exactly?

At first, you got fooled by someone, but after that, you made a fool of someone.

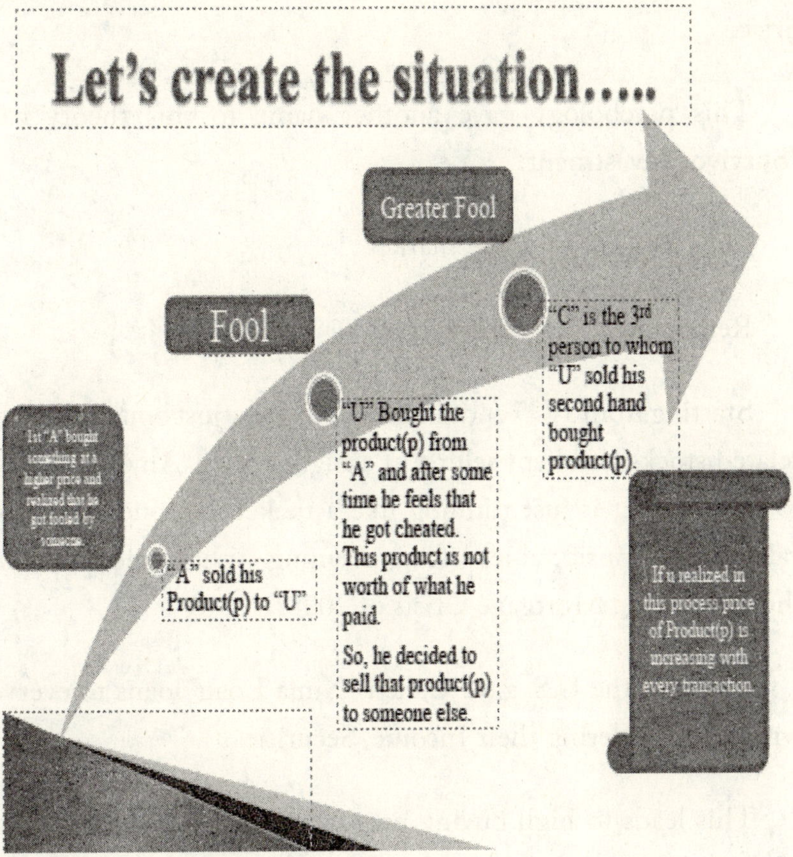

What does Greater Fools Theory say??

Greater Fools Theory says that price keeps rising because people are able to sell the overpriced product to someone without considering the valuation of the product.

That someone called **"Greater Fool."**

As I explained earlier. You may be noticed that after realizing that they bought the overpriced product, they try to recover the loss by selling at least at the same price or trying to sell at a higher price.

This psychology gave another name to this theory called "Survivor Investment."

Let's connect with the market.

Remember.Com bubble of 2000?

Starting from 1995 ends in 2000, everyone just bought Internet-related stocks and kept selling at a higher price. Any stock related to the internet is just running like a rocket. No one cared about valuation; intrinsic values left no meaning at that time. Remember the Sub-Prime Mortgage Crisis of 2008?

Banks in the U.S. gave Called "Ninja Loan" loans to everyone without considering their Income, Securities.

This leads to high buying pressure in real estate. This further leads to a rise in house prices. People keep buying houses and selling houses at a higher prices. Soon, people realized that they were not able to pay back loans.

This leads to a sudden fall in the price of houses. This leads to a recession globally. Currently, the Great Fool Theory is active in the case of Crypto Currencies. People are buying without knowing the valuations and basics of that. I always used to say in my videos, "First learn, then think to Earn."

Stock Picking Using Technical Analysis

So, as we studied the basic and advanced topic of Technical Analysis. Now is the time to apply the concepts:

Our first step would be to filter some fundamentally good stocks; then, we need to analyze them as per our technical analysis parameters.

Currently, we have around 7,462 companies listed on the National Stock Exchange and the Bombay Stock Exchange in the financial year 2021, as per the data given by statista.com.

It is not practically possible to track, analyze and trade all the stocks.

So, I am going to tell you a few ways with which you can select the stocks for intraday trading.

I always used to talk about price action trading in my videos.

So, I'll you the stock picking process based on:

1. Stocks price action

2. Without chart

3. Sectors trend

4. Candle pattern

5. Gap Approach

Stock Price Action: Under the strategy, you need to find the stock based on its price action movement. We can find both bullish and bearish stocks with this approach.

1st, find the stocks trading near an all-time or 52-week high in first 5 or 15 minute. You need to find this on the chart, or you can also get this on Moneycontrol.com

Select the top 5 companies.

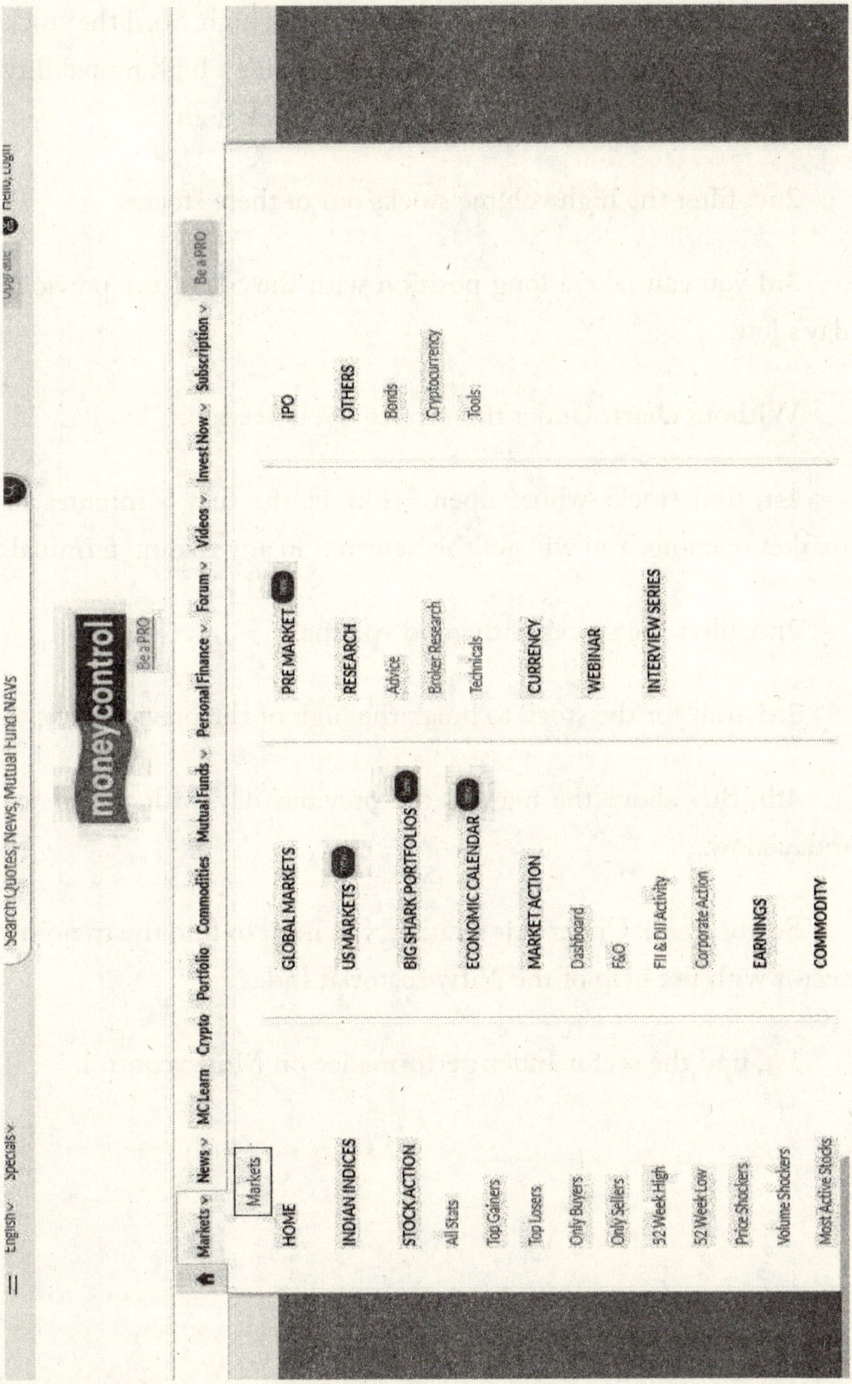
Search Quotes, News, Mutual Fund NAVs
moneycontrol
Be a PRO
Markets
News
MC Learn
Crypto
Portfolio
Commodities
Mutual Funds
Personal Finance
Forum
Videos
Invest Now
Subscription
Be a PRO
HOME
INDIAN INDICES
STOCK ACTION
All Stats
Top Gainers
Top Losers
Only Buyers
Only Sellers
52 Week High
52 Week Low
Price Shockers
Volume Shockers
Most Active Stocks
GLOBAL MARKETS
US MARKETS
BIG SHARK PORTFOLIOS
ECONOMIC CALENDAR
MARKET ACTION
Dashboard
F&O
FII & DII Activity
Corporate Action
EARNINGS
COMMODITY
PRE MARKET
RESEARCH
Advice
Broker Research
Technicals
CURRENCY
WEBINAR
INTERVIEW SERIES
IPO
OTHERS
Bonds
Cryptocurrency
Tools

It takes so much effort to touch a 52-week high. So, if the stock price reaches near 52-week or all-time high, it's a high probability that the stock may hit all time high or 52-week high.

2nd, filter the high volume stocks out of these stocks.

3rd you can take a long position with the SL of the previous day's low.

Without chart: Under this strategy, you need to:

1st, find stocks whose open = low in the first 5 minutes of market opening. You will get this screener in any trading terminal.

2nd, filter the stocks with good volume.

3rd, wait for the stock to break the high of the previous day.

4th, Buy above the high of the previous day, with the SL of today's low.

Sector trend: Under this strategy, you need to find the trending sector with the help of the Nifty sectorial Index.

1st, find the sector Index performance on Moneycontrol.

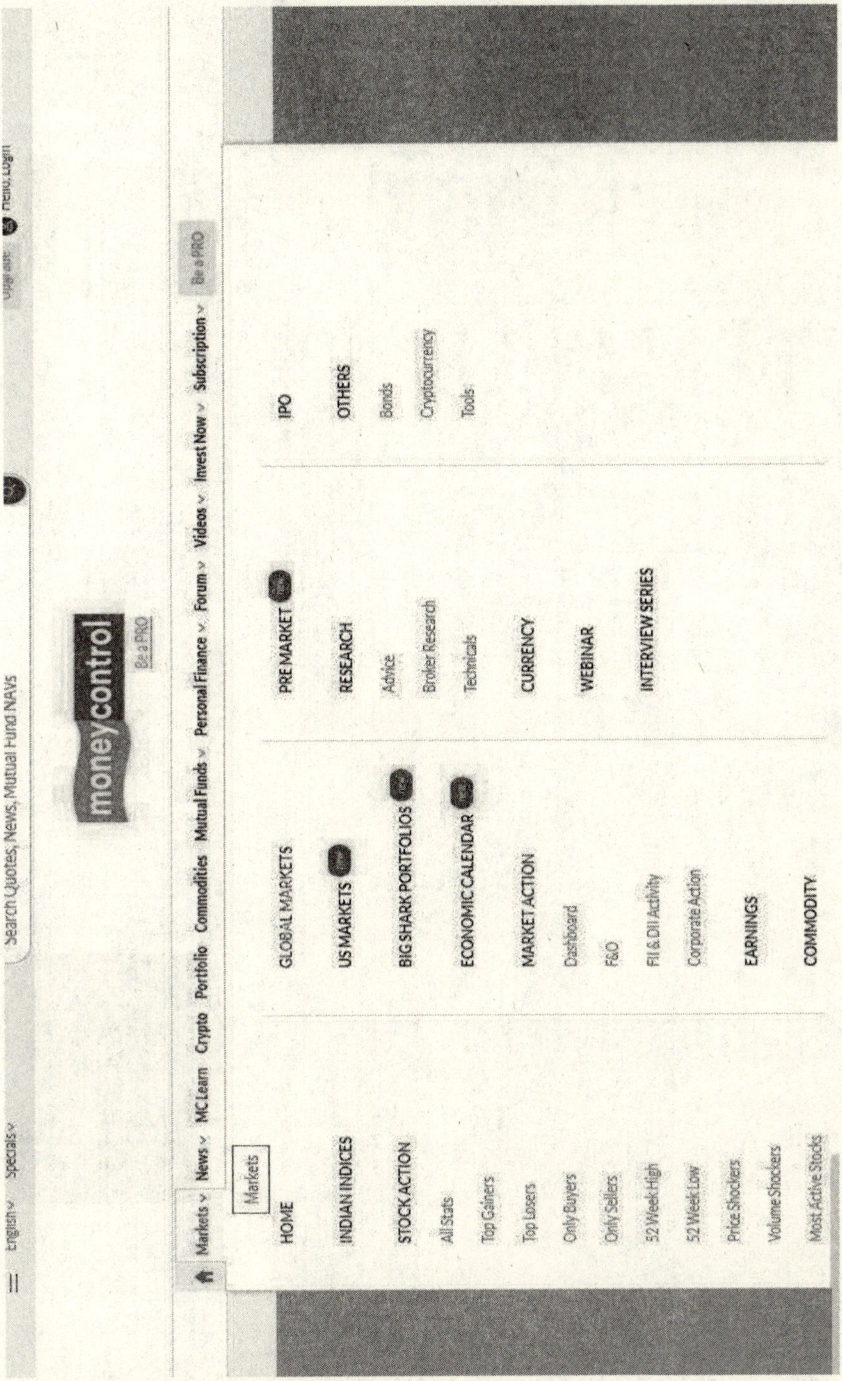
English ∨ Specials ∨
Search Quotes, News, Mutual Fund NAVs
Hello, Login
moneycontrol
Be a PRO
Markets ∨ News ∨ MCLearn Crypto Portfolio Commodities Mutual Funds ∨ Personal Finance ∨ Forum ∨ Videos ∨ Invest Now ∨ Subscription ∨ Be a PRO
Markets
HOME
INDIAN INDICES
STOCK ACTION
All Stats
Top Gainers
Top Losers
Only Buyers
Only Sellers
52 Week High
52 Week Low
Price Shockers
Volume Shockers
Most Active Stocks
GLOBAL MARKETS
US MARKETS
BIG SHARK PORTFOLIOS
ECONOMIC CALENDAR
MARKET ACTION
Dashboard
F&O
FII & DII Activity
Corporate Action
EARNINGS
COMMODITY
PRE MARKET
RESEARCH
Advice
Broker Research
Technicals
CURRENCY
WEBINAR
INTERVIEW SERIES
IPO
OTHERS
Bonds
Cryptocurrency
Tools

2nd, Select the best performing index.

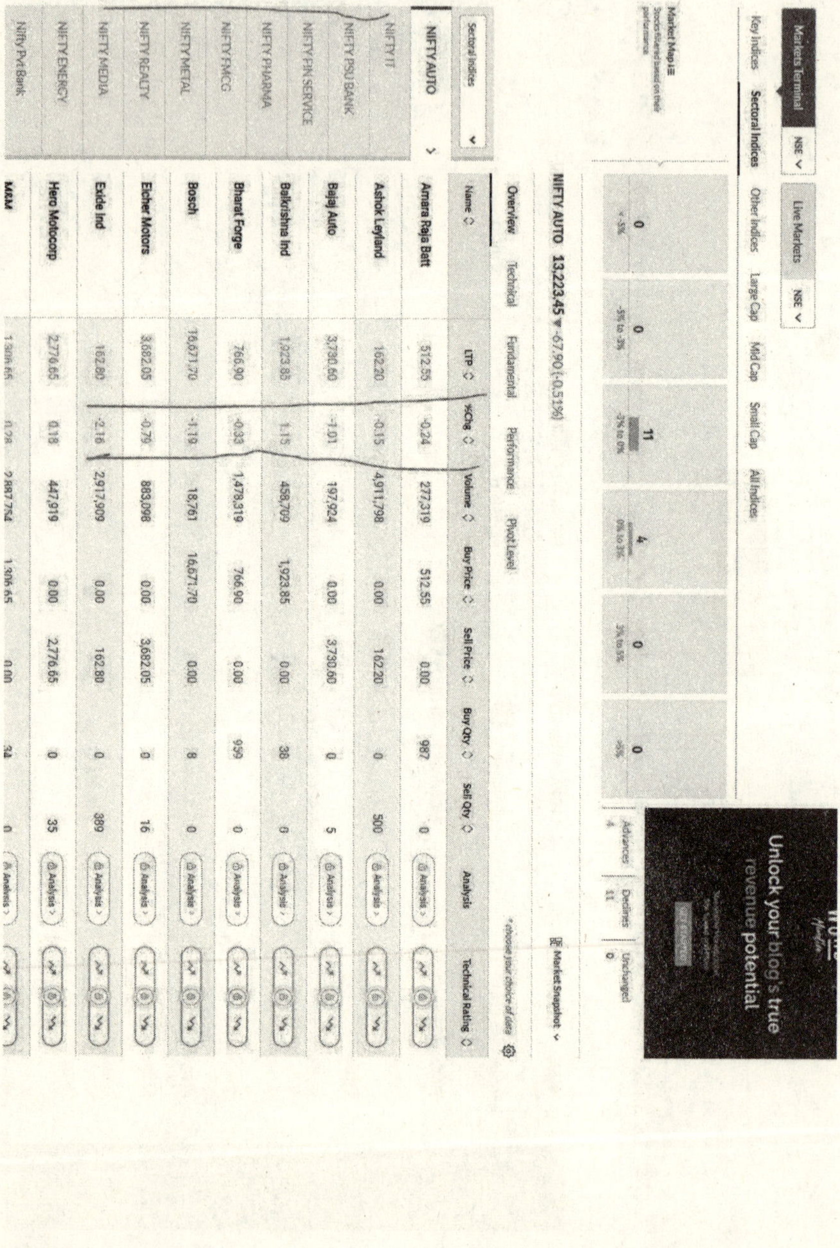

You can consider the best-performing index by checking the % change of the index.

3rd, after selecting the best performing index, perform a price action filter or without chart strategy on stock under the best performing index.

Candle Pattern: Do you remember the reversal candle we talked about in the candle stick chapter?

Those candles will give you the trade.

1st step is to find those reversals candles in stocks in first 5 minute of market opening. For that, you can use moneycontrol. com.

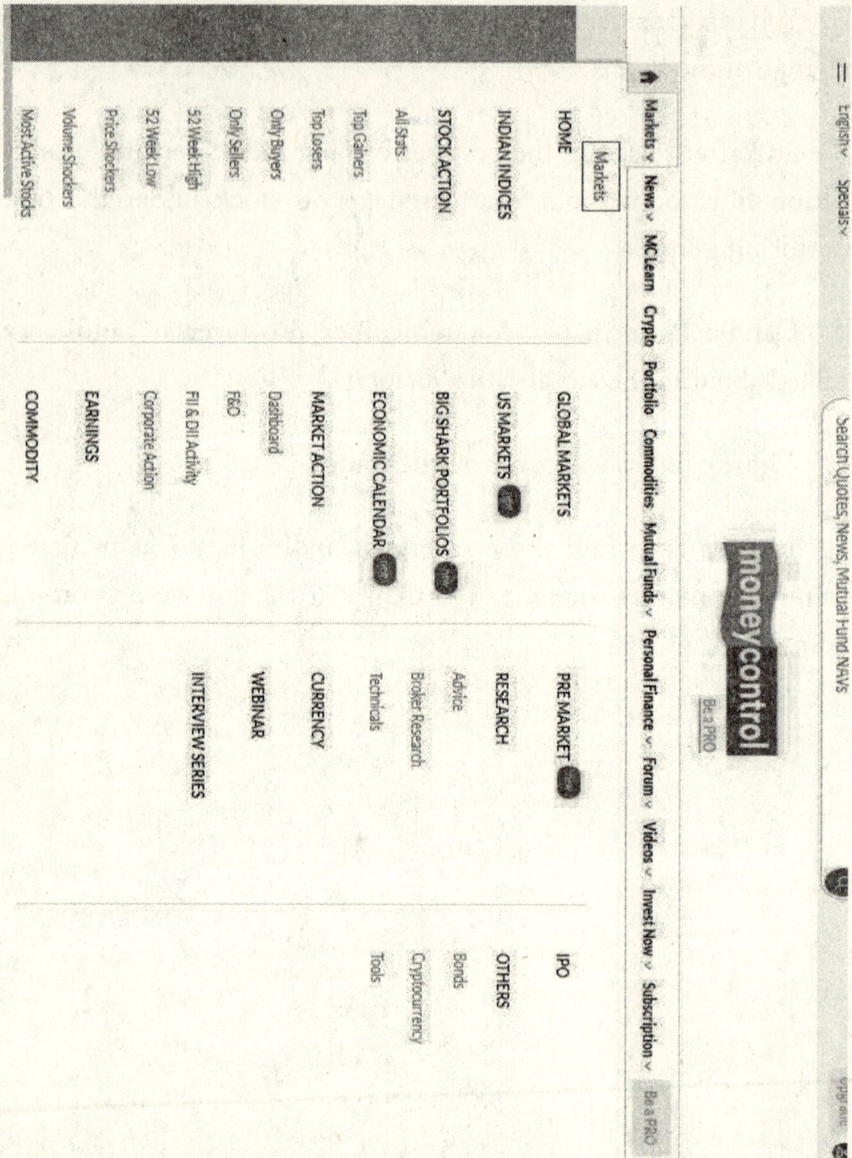
English Specials
Search Quotes, News, Mutual Fund NAVs
moneycontrol
Be a PRO
Hello, Login
Markets News MCLearn Crypto Portfolio Commodities Mutual Funds Personal Finance Forum Videos Invest Now Subscription
Be a PRO
Markets
HOME
INDIAN INDICES
STOCK ACTION
All Stats
Top Gainers
Top Losers
Only Buyers
Only Sellers
52 Week High
52 Week Low
Price Shockers
Volume Shockers
Most Active Stocks
GLOBAL MARKETS
US MARKETS
BIG SHARK PORTFOLIOS
ECONOMIC CALENDAR
MARKET ACTION
Dashboard
F&O
FII & DII Activity
Corporate Action
EARNINGS
COMMODITY
PRE MARKET
RESEARCH
Advice
Broker Research
Technicals
CURRENCY
WEBINAR
INTERVIEW SERIES
IPO
OTHERS
Bonds
Cryptocurrency
Tools

In the market section, you will find the sub-section technical.

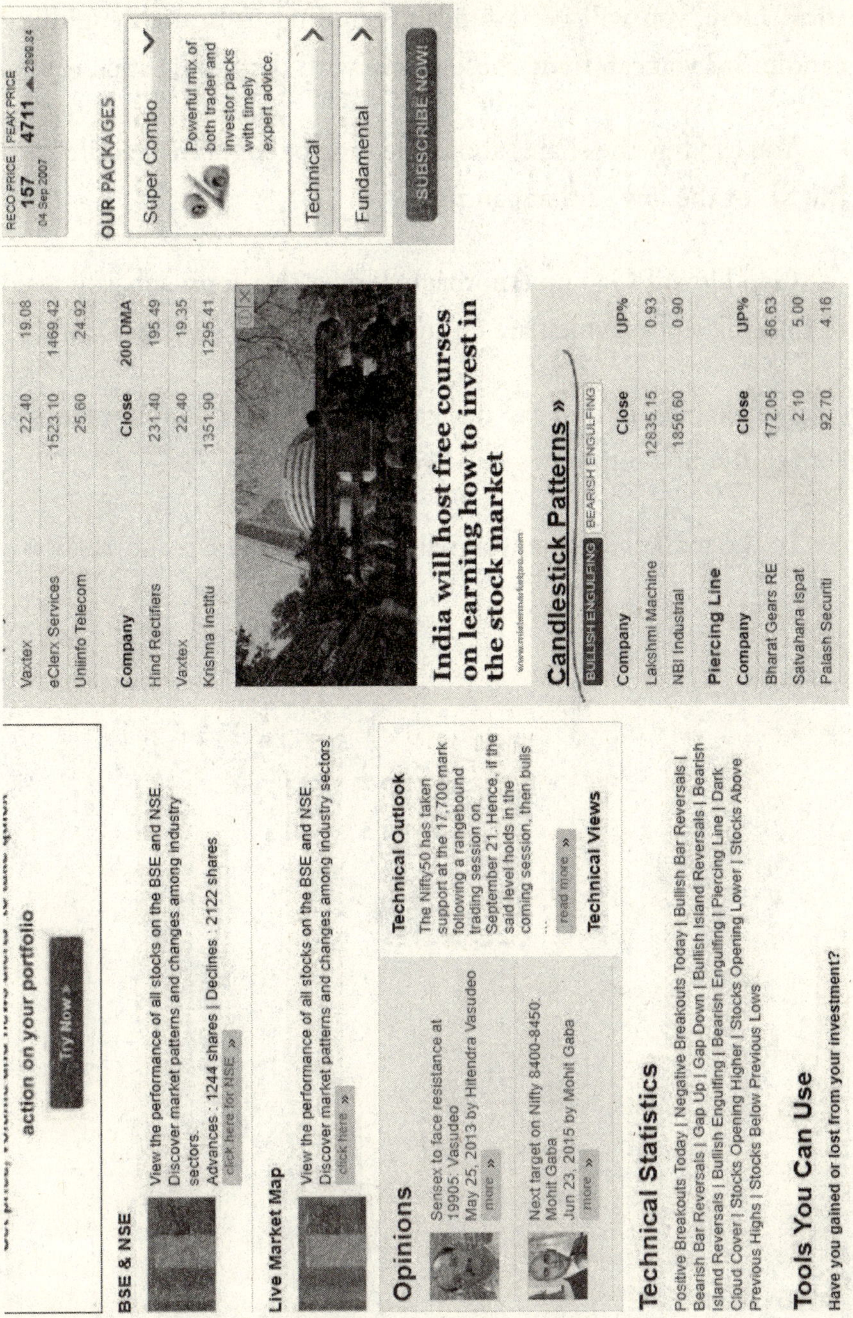

2nd Under technical, you will find stocks based on a candle stick. Here, you will get a bullish engulfing or bearish engulfing candle. 3rd you can trade these stocks with the candle stick rule.

You can buy the shares above the high of engulfing candle with the SL of the low of that candle.

Gap Down/ Gap up Approach: Under this approach, you need to find the stocks which are either in Gap Up or in Gap Down.

1st you have to find gap up/ gap down stocks on moneycontrol.com in the first 5 minutes in a live market.

In the market section, you will get Technical as a sub-section

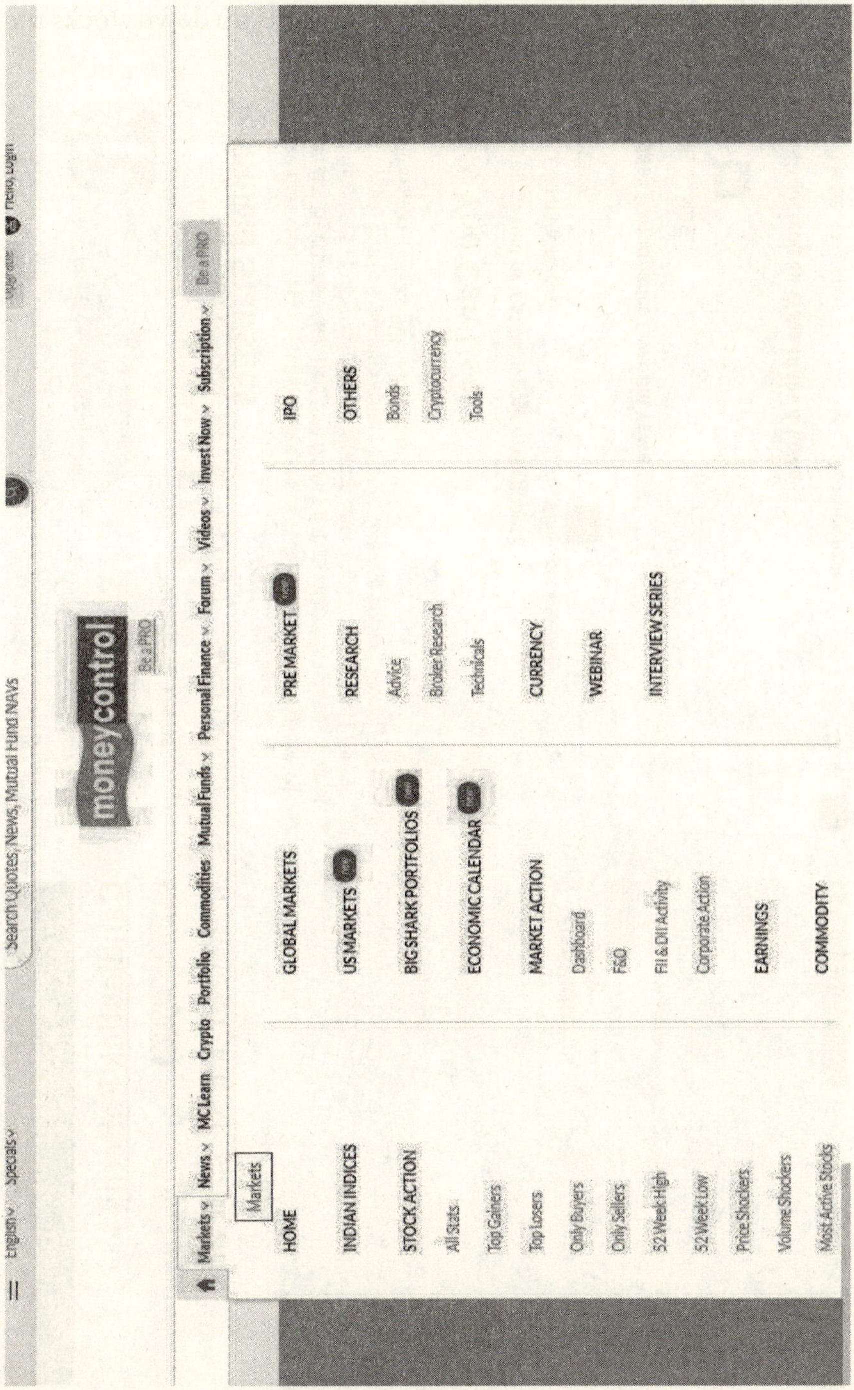
English ∨ Specials ∨
Search Quotes, News, Mutual Fund NAVs
moneycontrol
Be a PRO
Markets ∨ News ∨ MC Learn Crypto Portfolio Commodities Mutual Funds ∨ Personal Finance ∨ Forum ∨ Videos ∨ Invest Now ∨ Subscription ∨
Be a PRO
Markets
HOME
INDIAN INDICES
STOCK ACTION
All Stats
Top Gainers
Top Losers
Only Buyers
Only Sellers
52 Week High
52 Week Low
Price Shockers
Volume Shockers
Most Active Stocks
GLOBAL MARKETS
US MARKETS
BIG SHARK PORTFOLIOS
ECONOMIC CALENDAR
MARKET ACTION
Dashboard
F&O
FII & DII Activity
Corporate Action
EARNINGS
COMMODITY
PRE MARKET
RESEARCH
Advice
Broker Research
Technicals
CURRENCY
WEBINAR
INTERVIEW SERIES
IPO
OTHERS
Bonds
Cryptocurrency
Tools

Under technical, you will get a gap up and gap down stocks the below candle stick pattern

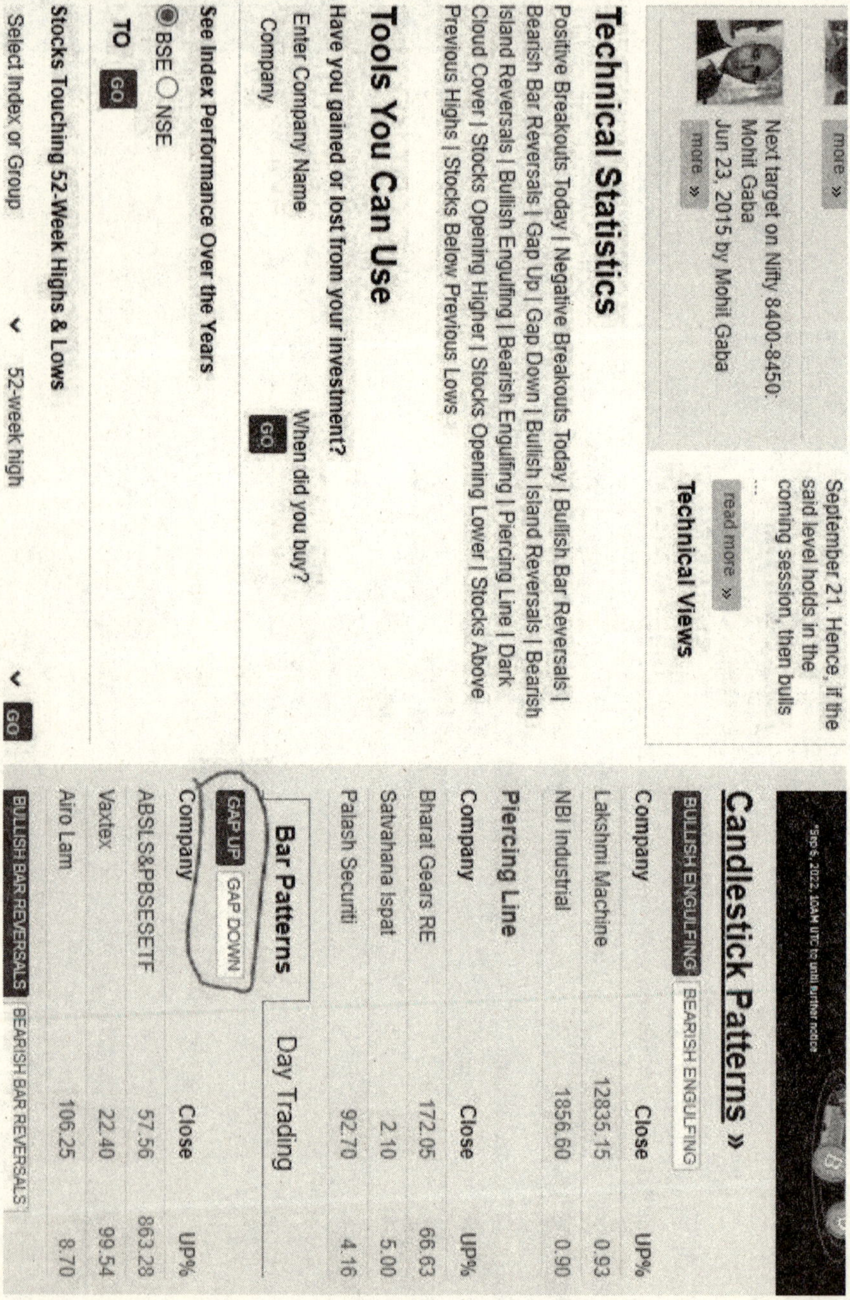

2nd you have to check if the market is bullish or bearish.

3rd you need to filter the stock of the opposite trend, which means If the market is bullish, you need to track gap-down stocks.

If the market is bearish, you need to track gap-up stocks.

4th, you need to make the opposite trade.

If the market is bullish and somehow the stock opens a gap down, there is a high probability that the stock may recover. Because most of the time, stocks follow the market trend.

In case of a gap down, you can buy the share above today's high, with the SL of today's low.

In case of a gap up, you can sell the share below today's low, with the SL of today's high.

These are the few techniques that you can use to pick the stock for intraday. Ample strategies are available in the market for stock picking.

But what works best?

The one at which you have command. The one on which you did ample practice.

You must have heard a quote, "Practice makes a man perfect." That's utterly applicable in the case of trading.

You must try and try a strategy that works for you.

In which you are comfortable doing an experiment to explore more around that strategy.

With this, we come to the end of the topic of stock picking.

Risk Management

Most crucial and less explained topic ever. I'll try to explain in a much easier way. If you notice, everything around us involves some risk. When I say every, I mean everything, from childhood to adulthood.

Anywhere and everywhere, you have surrounded the risk. To relate this, you first need to understand the core concept of risk.

What is Risk?

Risk is uncertainty. Yes, you have read it right. Risk is all about uncertain outcomes.

Now, I want your focus on understanding the concept.

When you know something is going to happen, that's no risk.

Risk is when you don't know what is going to happen. That's uncertainty, and confusion is defined as a Risk.

When you step out of your home, you don't know whether you will come back or not.

When you sleep at night, you don't know whether you will wake up or not. These uncertainties are defined as risks. When outcomes are not in your control. If you realize that we hardly have something whose outcomes are in our control. We even don't know exactly about our next step.

Everything is a prediction or assumption. Nothing is sure shot or called guaranteed. Even if we can predict the outcomes', that is called expected outcomes. But still, the risk is there.

If I try to summarize the above line, we are surrounded by uncertainty, so we are surrounded by risk.

When we predict the outcomes and expect something good, we generally cannot consider this a risk. But when we predict the negative outcomes', we consider this a risk.

So, as of now, you must understand that risk is all about uncertain adverse outcomes. Or if we predict the adverse outcomes. We can differentiate this into two types.

Expected Loss: This is what we had predicted and already expected. Not surprising.

Unexpected Loss : This is the excess of what we expect, which is surprising and defined as an unexpected loss.

Why I used the term loss?

Because, as I said, we consider only adverse outcomes as a Risk. And in finance, when we talk about adverse outcomes, it is viewed as a loss, what we as an individual or a firm predict.

If we connect this concept with investment or trading, market participants are generally more concerned about adverse outcomes than positive outcomes.

There is an inverse relationship between risk and reward.

In trading, to get more rewards, you need to take more risks.

Everyone wants to earn more, and for that, they need to take more risks. As I said, we cannot control outcomes, but we can manage them.

This is termed Risk Management.

We can always analyze the risk in terms of reward. Always remember we cannot avoid risk, but we can always manage risk.

We must decide actions to manage the risk in terms of the reward.

This relation between Risk and Reward has termed the Risk to Reward ratio: which tells us how much risk is taken for how much reward.

The list of actions in which we decide to manage risk is known as the Risk Management process.

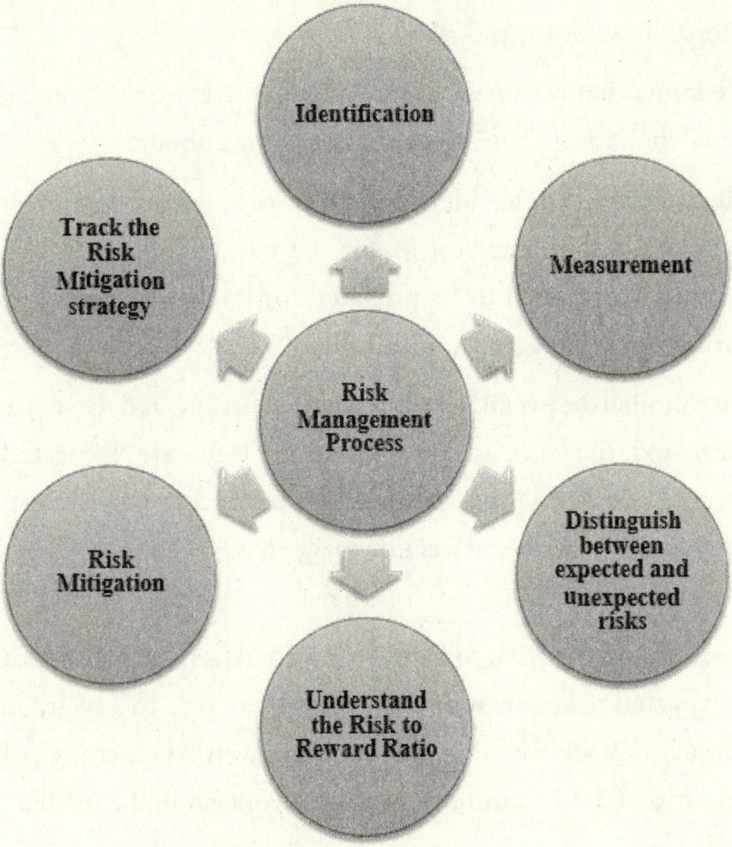

These are the Risk Management processes.

Let's understand every point:

Identification: The first step is to identify the risk. Risk identification is defined in many ways.

To manage the risk, we first should know if the risk is there or not; hence this is defined as Known Risk.

There are some risks that we don't know about; you can relate this with Covid19, no one expected this type of risk. So, this is considered an Unknown Risk.

We know that we are surrounded by risk every time. Some risks we know about and some risks we don't know about.

Measurement: After identifying the risk, we need to measure the density and frequency of loss if the risk is known. In case of unknown risk, we need to be prepared for any worst outcomes by measuring our risk absorption capacity.

Distinguish between Expected and Unexpected Risk: After we measured the risk, we now need to bifurcate Expected or unexpected risk. If the risk is expected, we need to prepare for the expected loss, and if the risk is unexpected, we need to be prepared with an emergency fund.

Understand the Risk to Reward Ratio: After the identification of the expected risk, now we need to check the risk-to-reward ratio. How much risk are we taking to get the reward? Generally risk to reward ratio of 1:1 is a minimum that anyone should consider.

Risk Mitigation: After identification, measurement, distinguishing, and risk- reward, now it's time to mitigate the risk. Practically, we cannot mitigate the risk entirely. Either we absorb the risk, or we can transfer the risk. These two are the most used strategy to mitigate risk.

Track the Risk Mitigation Strategy: After all the steps, we now need to track the risk mitigation strategies. Whether is it going smoothly or not?

Now, let's connect all the risk management concepts with trading.

Risk Management in Trading

Like every business, trading is also surrounded by risks. Risk of a significant loss.

Risk of losing trading capital.

Risk of losing profits.

Risk of losing peace of Mind.

Risk management helps in all the points mentioned above.

Before dealing with these points, you need to check yourself first. You need to know yourself.

Because in finance, the risk is a subjective topic as per individual.

For example: Taking the risk of losing Rs.2 lakh is bearable for you but might not be bearable for me. So, in that case, the risk measurement is different for both of us.

So, you need to know your risk profile.

Identify the risk profile.

You must know a few things about yourself to identify your

risk profile. Like: Risk Appetite : It is nothing but the amount you are willing to keep at risk. In one line, if I say this is the amount you can afford to lose without hesitation. It is influenced by your financial background.

Risk Tolerance: It is your capacity for risk absorption when deviating from the risk appetite. It may sound similar to Risk Appetite, but it is not. Risk appetite means how much you are willing to lose in trading, but risk tolerance is like how much loss you can tolerate above your risk appetite.

Let's see an example: You have Rs. 10 lakh in your trading capital.

Out of which, your risk appetite allows you to bear a loss of Rs. 2 Lakh. If the loss exceeds Rs. 2 Lakh. Up to which you can afford to handle.

Let's say you can handle a loss till 4 Lakhs, at max. That is your risk tolerance.

Trading strategy : You need to see which trading strategy you prefer. High-risk, high-reward strategy, Low risk, low reward strategy High risk, low reward strategy with high probability Low risk, high reward strategy with low probability You need to decide which strategy suits you.

Personality: Your personality plays a very crucial role in trading. If you are a risk taker, you may prefer a high-risk reward trading strategy. You have to choose a trading strategy based on your behavior.

Time Frame : You need to check which time frame suits you best. Like if your strategy works best intraday, it means a one-day time frame is best for you. You need to decide whether you are an intraday trader or a positional trader.

So, now you have identified your risk profile, let's understand how you can evaluate the trading risk.

By the term evaluate the risk I mean to say that:

How do you decide your position?

How to calculate Stop Loss and Target with proper risk reward ratio. We already know that market moves in trend.

So, we need to take trade only when the trend is clear, stocks pass your stock picking criteria, and all the indicators indicate the same signal.

In this case, you can use your 20% trading capital; always remember never to use 100% of your capital in one trade. 20% is the maximum you can use in one trade, with the risk reward of 1:2.

Likewise: Find at least five bullish stocks and execute the trade only when all the criteria will meet, and deploy 20% of your trading capital on each stock with the risk-reward ratio of 1:2.

These stocks are filtered through price action strategies. So, all these trades would be highly probable because, after price action, you have executed the trade when indicators confirm. This is how you can evaluate your position with high probability trading.

Whenever there is confusion about trends or anything which gives you doubt in your trade, you still want to take the risk; in that case, use only 10% of your capital.

Let me summarize this for you; it is very simple to understand:

You can either buy shares worth Rs. 100 and sell them at 110 to earn Rs. 10. this has a very low probability.

Or you can buy ten shares of Rs. 10 and sell them at 101 to earn Rs. 10. this has a high probability.

In both cases, you will earn Rs. 10 only, but you have to evaluate which suits you. Trading low probability but high reward trade, the low trading probability with the same reward. So, it is easy to decide as per the rule mentioned in the book. If all the criteria allow trading, then take the risk; if not, avoid the risk, and go with the low-risk strategy.

How to set Stop Loss and Target?

Many trading setups I discussed in the book are based on the trend line, price action, and indicators.

Whenever any trading setups trigger a trade, it is vital to know the levels to exit the trade.

In fact, you must have heard this before that you should know whether to exit the trade before entering the trade.

Exit the trades means both exits on Stop loss and exit on target. Let's understand the term Stop Loss and target.

Stop Loss: Focus on the name; it is the tool to stop the loss-making trades. Let's understand with the help of an example:

You got a trade-in ABC stock at Rs. 100, Now, what will be the exit strategy?

You have invested Rs. 100, and your risk appetite is Rs. 20, which means if the share fall below 80, you will exit the trade.

In this case, you exit the trade based on your risk appetite.

The price below which your risk appetite will not allow you to be in trade. It is called a Stop Loss price. You need to cut your loss at this level.

You can place stop loss in many ways like:

Based on your risk appetite, as I explained above.

Based on your trading setup, like suppose you are trading based on RSI, your trading setup is that If RSI coss above 60, you can and hold till RSI comes below

57. This will be your SL based on RSI. Likewise, you can use this in all trading setups.

Target: It is the price at which you have decided to make a profit. It generally depends on your trading setup. Like, let's suppose you are trading on RSI, and your trading setup is to Buy when RSI is above 60 and Target is when RSI is at 70.

Another setup to set a target would be support and resistance, which you can find with the help of Fibonacci levels.

For example, you bought a share at Rs. 100, with the first resistance of Rs. 130. In that case, Rs. 130 will be your Target price.

Now Stop Loss and Target together.

A few things which you need to consider before deciding on stop loss and target price are:

You need to filter a trade with a high probability with at least a risk-reward ratio of 1:2. Which means your SL should be Rs. 1 and Reward should be Rs. 2. So, that out of 10 trades, if you lost 6 also, you will lose, Rs. 6 but in 4 trades you made Rs. 8, which brings you in net profit of Rs. 2, even after your 60% trades are wrong.

By high probability, I mean to say that all the criteria mentioned in the book should approve the trade.

Because trading is a game of probability, you have to increase your probability of winning.

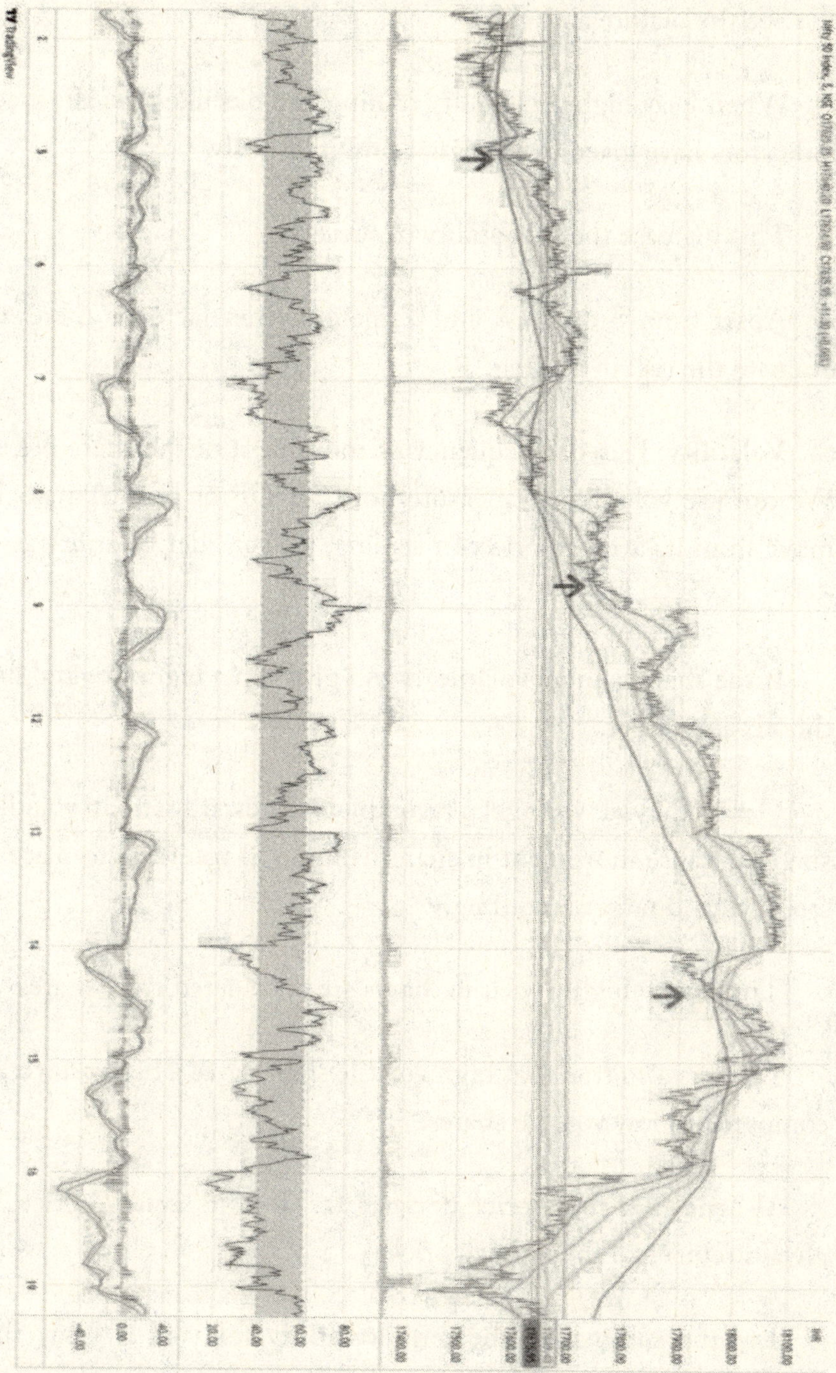

See the picture above.

When I say high probability trading, it looks like this; all three indicators have given a buy signal simultaneously.

This increase the probability of success.

Apart from Stop Loss and Target, another factor is there to evaluate the risk in trading.

Volatility: It is the frequency of movement of the share price. We can use volatility to measure how far (UP or Down) a stock move from its average price. In trading, we consider volatility as a risk.

If the share is more volatile, it will give you a big move and hit the SL and target.

Generally, you won't get a favorable risk-reward ratio in volatile shares because movement in shares is high, so you need to place a stop loss and target accordingly.

That's why highly volatile shares are considered risky shares.

But it is also true that high volatile shares give a high return as compared to low volatile shares.

Whenever a share price deviates far from its average price, it always returns to the average price.

Let me summarize the term volatility for you; if I say the

volatility of a stock is 2%, it means the stock might move Up or down 2% from its average price. We need to be careful before placing a stop loss and target orders that if a stock can move 2% in either direction, so, if you placed a target above 2%, it might not hit, and SL below 2%, it might hit.

So, here we are, done with evaluating the trading part.

I have not touched anything which we cannot use in trading daily. Because I don't believe in theories. Only the practical approach works.

Now I would like to highlight some of the popular risk management strategies which most traders are using in trading.

1. Do proper back testing before following any trading setup: I discussed many trading setups in the book; you need to understand that every trading setup has some rules which need to be followed then only it make money for you. When you decide to follow any trading setup, it's your responsibility to do back testing to check the performance of the trading setups and whether this setup suits you or not. When you find a setup that satisfies your return expectation and also syncs with your trading personality, that setup will make you money.

2. Follow the position seizing rule: As I have mentioned in the section "How to decide trading position," never deploy all the capital in one trade.

3. Have Patience: As I said about high probability trading opportunities, you will not get so quickly; you need to be disciplined and keep patience till your trading setups give you a signal to trade.

4. Follow strict Stop Loss and Target levels: As I explained in the

Stop loss section. You can decide the stop based on your risk appetite or may be based on trading setups; in both cases, it is essential to follow the levels. Don't let greed and fear control your trading. I'll discuss this in further detail in the psychology chapter.

5. Keep Trailing Stop Loss: Heard a new term? Well, yes, I have not discussed Trailing Sl earlier for a reason because I want you to remember this, it will enhance your trading setups and winning rates. It is a modified version of SL., which keeps moving as per fix % or as fix points as you decide. Let's say you have taken a trade at Rs. 100, with the SL of 80 and a target of 130, with a trailing SL of 5 Point as the price moves 10 points up; it means when the stock price reach 110, your Sl will shift to 85 from 90 if the stock price reached at 120, SL will shift to 90 from 85, it continues till the target price. Trailing SL will help in locking the loss as well as locking the profit.

6. Avoid margin trading: This is the most important topic of risk management. Margin trading is defined as leveraged trading in which you can borrow funds from the broker, up to 5 times your fund to trade. This feature acts as a two-way knife. Sometimes it helps, but most of the time, it hurts your financials. You must have heard this line from your elders "Jitna Chaadar h Utna hi pair pasaaro." Personally, I don't believe in these lines because I believe in "Chaadar bara karna" instead of pair km pasaarna. But when it comes to trading, I strongly believe in this line. I talked about risk appetite and risk tolerance in the risk profiling section. Leverage trading might violate your risk appetite and risk tolerance. You may get attracted by your broker when they say that you can buy five times more than your fund and earn extra profit, but with that, remember that there is a risk involved in every trade, so you incur a loss, and you may lose more than your fund.

7. Choose your stock broker wisely: It might seem like not so helpful point but believe me, it is essential to go with a broker who has credibility in the market. Remember the crises of Karvy Stock Broking, the data leaked issue of Zerodha, and many more examples are available in the news if you find them. Don't focus just on low brokerage but also on service. With a long credible track record.

TRADING PSYCHOLOGY

You must have heard that trading is 20% dependent on setup and 80% dependent on the psychology of the traders.

As I said, in risk management in trading also, you must have patience in trading; you need to follow the rules.

Psychology is all about the study of the human mind and behavior scientifically. Similarly, Trading psychology studies the thoughts and feelings influencing whether a trader will succeed or fail. Different facets of a person's personality and habits that affect their trading activities are represented by trading psychology.

Therefore, trading psychology can be just as crucial to success as other factors like information, experience, and competence.

We have learned many factors of trading, from basics to advance. Like all the other factors, psychology is also a crucial factor in trading.

Let's understand this with an example: Suppose you had executed a trade at 100 with an SL of 80 and a target of 140.

See how your psychology may affect your trade.

Normal rules say that you have to exit the trade either at 80 or 140.

But when the price hits 140, you may think that it may touch 150 also. This greed holds you from profit booking in the hope of more profit.

When the price hits 80, you may think it may recover above the SL, and you will not incur loss and hold the position in the hope of recovery. This is your fear which holds you from booking a loss.

In case of greed, to earn more profit, you hold the position for a long time even after your target price is reached; this might work for some time, but not always; there is a high probability that stock price may fall till the SL price after hitting the target price.

In case of fear, to reduce the loss, you hold the position for a long time in the hope of recovery even after your SL price is reached; this might work for some time, but not always; there is a high probability that stock price may fall further after breaking the SL price.

Two of the most essential elements of trading psychology are discipline and risk- taking. A trader's ability to put these elements into practice is essential to the success of his or her trading strategy. Thoughts like hope and regret also play a part in trading behavior; fear and greed are frequently linked to trading psychology.

Till now, we have already studied that Technical analysis is the study or price movement of securities; the reason for that price movement is demand and supply, which market participants generate. Market participants are human, and humans have emotions that create the feeling of Greed and Fear.

Greed wants you to imagine more money. Fear wants to reduce the loss.

Both are led by human behavior.

When one has devoted a sizable amount of time, energy, and money to advancing or supporting a specific point of view or method of market analysis, it is very difficult to adapt or be flexible. Because of this, it is particularly challenging for directional traders to follow the constantly changing course of price action. We refer to a trader or analyst as being in a condition of cognitive dissonance when they start to feel uneasy or anxious when faced with contradictory facts.

The trader or analyst will make an effort to lessen this uneasy state of dissonance by either limiting their information intake to that which supports or conforms to their view of the market or by making an effort to rationalize away the issue. Any alternative news, analysis, newsletter, or article is easily discounted or rejected if the trader resorts to simply exposing themselves to information that supports the widely recognized perspective or analysis of the market.

For instance, once a trader is confident that a certain market is bullish, there is a propensity to disregard indications that do not support this belief.

Bullish outlook the trader may also start to mentally divide information into separate categories so as to lessen the overall impact of conflicting information by mentally containing and diluting the threat.

In the face of overwhelming bearishness, the trader may also choose to limit their attention to only the positive parts of the market. Only information that supports the trader's view of the market is selectively perceived, and the trader may even interpret information incorrectly in order to make it consistent with his or her current expectations.

In other words, traders rarely make trading decisions based on what they observe happening in the market. Instead, they favor trading based on what they anticipate will happen in the markets. Therefore, trader and investor expectations are the main factors that influence the market.

Understand the concept of trading psychology

Now try to understand the concept of trading psychology.

Trading psychology can be connected to a few particular feelings and actions acting frequently act as market trading triggers.

Most emotional trading is typically attributed to either greed or fear in conventional descriptions of emotionally motivated conduct in markets.

Greed can be defined as an over whelming desire for gain that, at times, interferes with reason and judgment.

Therefore, this description of the greed-inspired investor or irrational trader presupposes that the feeling of greed can influence traders to engage in various unfavorable behaviors.

This could be engaging in over trading, high-risk trading, purchasing stock in an unproven business or technology simply because its price is rising quickly, or purchasing shares without doing any due diligence on the underlying venture.

On the other hand, fear makes traders end positions too soon or decide not to take risks due to worries about significant losses. As I mentioned above, fears hold your position in the hope of recovery.

Fear, a strong emotion that can make traders and investors act irrationally in their haste to abandon the market, is evident during downturns.

Fear frequently develops into panic, and panic selling typically results in severe market selloffs.

A trader may enter a trade out of regret after first passing it up because the stock moved too quickly.

This breach of trading discipline frequently leads to direct losses from declining securities prices from peak highs.

Let's discuss human psychology

Greed: When you crave excessive gains, greed sets in. Your stock market riches won't be made in a day, just as Rome wasn't. If you find yourself winning consistently, take your money and run. The vast majority of the time, your greed will ruin a winning streak!

You ought to establish a predetermined profit booking level to thwart greed.

To prevent being influenced by greed, set your stop-loss and book-profit levels before you ever initiate a trade.

You have a good trading mindset when you are happy with your earnings and avoid chasing unreasonable profits.

Fear: We experience fear as a natural response when something is in danger. When trading, risks could take many different forms:

Several unfavorable stock or market news stories Fear of financial loss Realizing after placing a trade that it is not working out as you had hoped Traders overreact and tend to sell off their holdings out of panic. Conversely, when traders do not allow fear to influence their buy/sell approach, they have a good trading psyche.

Before trading, every trader needs to understand their fears and their motivations. Consider these issues to rapidly identify the problem and search for a solution.

Your main aim should be to avoid letting loss aversion prevent you from turning a profit.

Regret: Trading regret can come in two forms.

An unsuccessful trade could make a trader regret it.

Regret not making a trade that might have been successful.

Accepting that you cannot take advantage of every market chance is the best approach to prevent developing a regretful trading attitude. You may win some, and you lose some regarding the stock market.

Your trading psyche will automatically improve if you embrace this rule.

Hope: Investors frequently mistake trading with gambling.

They constantly expect to win and become discouraged when they don't.

You need a good trading mindset independent of hope if you want to succeed as a trader.

Your entire investment is in jeopardy if you keep hoping that things will improve soon.

Don't let hope keep you involved in a trade that will cost you money. Be sensible and record your losses when they are due.

You must put effort into developing a mindset if you want to become and remain successful as a trader.

How trading psychology plays a vital role in Technical Analysis.

Technical analysts who base their trade judgments on charting methods frequently need to consider trading psychology.

A variety of insights into a security's movement can be obtained from security charting.

Technical analysis and charting methods can help identify patterns for buying and selling opportunities. Still, it also requires an awareness of market movements and an intuition for them that is based on an investor's trading mentality.

Technical charting presents several situations where a trader must rely not just on the indication provided by the chart but also on their personal familiarity with the securities they are tracking and their hunch of how broader issues are impacting the market.

Traders who pay close attention to all of the factors that affect a security's price and those who are disciplined and confident have a healthy trading psyche that frequently leads to success.

In trading psychology, innate human traits like biases and emotions are crucial.

The primary goal of studying trade psychology is to increase one's awareness of the different dangers linked to bad psychological traits and to cultivate more positive traits.

Trading psychology experts typically do not operate out of bias or emotion. Therefore, they have a better possibility of making money while trading or, at the very least, of limiting their losses.

Understanding why people make irrational decisions in the market or with other financial matters is a part of trading psychology.

A branch of behavioral economics known as behavioral finance makes the case that investors and financial professionals' financial decisions are influenced by psychological factors and biases.

Furthermore, biases and effects can be used to explain various market anomalies, particularly those that occur in the stock market, such as sharp increases or decreases in stock prices.

Typically, behavioral finance includes the following ideas:

People often imitate the financial habits of the vast majority of the herd, according to the theory of **herd behavior.**

In the stock market, herding is infamous for causing crude rallies and sell-offs. In one line, "Following the crowd is a herd behavior."

Decision-making based on strong emotions or emotional strains, such as worry, wrath, fear, or enthusiasm, is known as the "emotional gap."

People frequently make irrational rational decisions as a result of their emotions. Your mood may impact your trading.

The propensity to base decisions on one's own knowledge or abilities is known as "Self-attribution."

Self-attribution frequently results from an innate talent for a specific skill. People frequently overrate their knowledge in this category higher than that of others.

The process of tying a budgetary level to a specific reference is known as "Anchoring."

Examples can include justifying spending based on various satisfaction utilities or spending consistently at a set budget level.

Buying shares as per your budget.

The search for penny stocks by novice traders and investors without considering the company's health might be attributed to anchoring. We must realize that quality comes at a cost.

How to Get In the Mindset of a Successful Trader

Frankly speaking, I personally don't believe in being in the mindset of successful traders. Mindset and Emotions are subjective and different for every individual. Knowing your own emotions, prejudices, and personality factors will make it easier for you to improve your trading psychology.

Once you are aware of these, you may create a trading strategy that takes them into consideration to lessen their potential impact on your choice-making.

For instance, instead of taking a slight loss on your trading account, you can choose to let losses accumulate in the hopes that the market will turn around. More significant losses or the eventual demise of your trading account could result from this.

You could use stops as a strategy to mitigate your losses and decide when to close a specific trade before you initiate the position to combat this.

By doing this, you have become mindful of your own prejudices and emotions because you have chosen to take action against them rather than act on them. Let me tell you some points that will improve your trading psychology if you follow.

Following the rules is more important than knowing the rule.

Know your personality characteristics: The ability to recognize your personality traits early on is one of the keys to building good trading psychology. You must be completely honest with yourself and acknowledge any impulsive inclinations or a propensity for irrational behavior.

In that case, it is imperative to control these tendencies while you are actively trading because they may induce you to make snap judgments that lack sufficient analytical support. Playing to your unique talents is crucial, though. For example, if you have a naturally cool-headed and strategic mentality, you can use these qualities to your advantage while trading.

Follow trading setups: Trading setups are essential to helping you reach your objectives. The blueprint for your trading, a trading setup should include your time commitments, available trading capital, risk-to-reward ratio, and a trading method you are at ease with.

A trading setup might specify that you'll dedicate an hour to trading every morning and evening and that you won't risk more than 2% of your portfolio's entire worth on any one trade. As the guidelines for opening or closing a trade are already marked for you, this can help you minimize losses and limit the impact of emotions on your trading.

Keep Patience: You must be patient with your position since patience is an essential component of the discipline. When you make decisions based on feelings

like fear, you might close a position too soon and lose money. Maintain your discipline and patience while having faith in your analyses. In the same way, it's crucial to be patient and wait for the proper time to enter a trade rather than do so immediately.

Possess a Solid Knowledge Base: Increasing your knowledge is one of the finest strategies to enhance your trading psyche. Being well-versed in stock market fundamentals is essential if you want to overcome a bad trading mindset.

Take Breaks: Stop for a while after a loss. Sometimes, rather than rushing into another trade to make up some of your losses, the best thing you can do after a loss is to step away from your trading account for a brief period of time to collect your thoughts and compose yourself.

The best traders are those who accept their losses and view them as opportunities for growth. Before returning to their platform, they will usually take a few minutes to themselves to reflect on what went wrong with that specific trade and try to avoid making the same error again.

Be confident but not overconfident: Quitting when you're ahead and taking your winnings is just as crucial as taking a break after a setback. You might feel invincible after a run of victories or one particularly sizable victory, at which point you might move into another position and try to repeat the process.

Since today is "your day" on the markets, you can even initiate a string of fresh positions hoping that none of them will lose money. Due to this, you can end up taking unwarranted risks or diversifying your portfolio too quickly without first researching each market.

During your time on the markets, happiness can be just as harmful as rage, so it's critical to recognize when it might be influencing your judgment or negatively affecting your trading mentality.

Maintain Trading Journal: You can keep track of all your wins and losses, as well as the feelings you had during each trade, by keeping a trading journal. As a result, it represents the conclusion of all the earlier ideas discussed in this essay. You can use it to determine whether or not the decisions you made at any given time were wise ones.

You can track when you decided to cut your losses and the final price the asset reached in your trading journal. You can determine if you made the proper choice or not by doing this. It can also be utilized to keep track of when you accepted your wins and whether your feelings affected whether you decided to close that position too soon or a little bit late.

Put the right frame of mind in place : Remember that markets are never stable before you even begin your trading day. You may have a good and bad time, but both will pass.

Giving yourself time is a powerful way to enhance your trading psychology. On your first trading day, you won't make much money.

You must invest time and energy in developing a trading technique unaffected by current market conditions. Even though emotions will always be a part of trading, the objective is to lessen the degree to which they influence your trading psyche.

Bonus

You must know that I always used to have some bonus for you. Similarly, as I explained everything about technical analysis.

Now, I will share some bonus tips which help you earn extra profit apart from regular trading.

IPO Analysis

IPO means Initial Public Offering; when any company wants to raise funds from the market, they offer the public to be a part owner of the company. By offering the shares of the company. It's the company's first public offering; that's why it is called an "Initial Public Offering."

You can earn extra profit by applying for IPO.

Generally, one lot of IPO is valued at Rs. 15000 and gives a reasonable return if the company is good.

Few questions you need to ask before applying for the IPO. Why did the business decide to go public?

What will the business do with the funds raised through the IPO?

What is the level of market competition for the goods or services the company offers?

What are the chances of the business expanding?

Corporate Action Analysis

Any action taken by an organization that impacts its stakeholders, such as its standard and preferred shareholders and bondholders, is referred to as a corporate action. The company's board of directors typically approves these events; however, some events may also be put to vote by shareholders. In addition, shareholders are required to respond to certain company acts.

Few general corporate actions:

Dividend: Common corporate actions that affect stock prices include cash dividends. A cash dividend is a distribution of earnings to a particular class of shareholders that the board must approve directors of a firm. For example, let's say the board of directors of business ABC decides to approve an Rs.2 cash dividend. Company ABC's stock price would reflect the corporate action on the ex-dividend date and be R. 2 lower than its prior closing price.

You can buy the bullish shares before the ex-dividend date and collect the dividend, and after, you can sell the shares at a higher price. This way, you can earn twice from the same stock.

Stock Split: Another typical corporate activity that modifies a company's existing shares is a stock split. A stock split entails an increase in the number of outstanding shares by a given multiple and a corresponding fall in share price. For instance, ONGC intended to split its stock seven to one in Sep 2022

As a result, while the number of outstanding shares increased, the share price of ONGC declined by a ratio of 7.

Despite a significant shift in stock price, the split had little impact on ONGC market capitalization.

Perhaps this may be a good time to buy the shares of a healthy company.

Rights Issue: When a firm does a rights issue, it only makes new or extra shares available to existing shareholders. Prior to the shares going on sale to the public, the current shareholders have the option to buy or receive them. A rights issue, which frequently takes the form of a stock split, can mean that existing shareholders are being given the opportunity to benefit from an exciting new development.

You must have a share of the company to benefit from the right issue. So, you can do two things: watch my videos regularly and track the corporate actions on the NSE/BSE site.

Bonus Issue: Free extra shares being offered to current shareholders is a bonus issue, often referred to as a scrip issue or a capitalization issue. As an alternative to raising the dividend payout, a firm may decide to distribute more shares. A firm might, for instance, provide one bonus share for every five shares held.

You can buy the shares before the ex-date to benefit from the bonus issue.

Bulk and Block Deal Analysis

When prominent market participants buy or sell company shares that are defined as a Bulk and Block deal.

Bulk Deal: A bulk deal is a transaction in which the total number of shares purchased or sold exceeds 0.5% of the outstanding shares of a publicly traded firm. Bulk transactions take place during the broker's regular trading window. Every time a transaction occurs, the broker managing the bulk deal trade must inform the stock exchanges of the specifics. Unlike block deals, bulk deal orders are open to the public view.

Block Deal: It is an agreement between two parties to buy or sell shares at a price that has been agreed upon, involving a minimum of 500,000 shares or a minimum transaction value of Rs. 5 crore. The transaction is conducted through a separate trading window, which runs from 9.15 to 9.50 am at the start of trading hours. There must be delivered in every exchange.

The cost of a share ordered at the window must be between 1% to 1% of the previous day's closing price or the current market price. Block deals take place in a separate window, making them invisible to the general market. However, the names of the company, the client, the number of shares, and the average price at which the trade occurred are all disclosed along with other information about the block deal orders on the bourse website.

Both bulk and block deals can give you an opportunity to generate extra income or may also act like a trading setup based on these deals.

Given the large sums necessary to engage in such transactions and the percentage of shares involved, it is typically deep-pocketed investors like fund houses, foreign institutional investors, banks, insurance companies, and HNIs.

Investors frequently use bulk and block transactions to assess the stock's significant shareholders' interests. When multiple stock transactions repeatedly occur over a period of time, it might be interpreted as a vote of confidence, and the stock price may climb soon as a result. However, a large organization or investor purchasing shares through such transactions does not guarantee that the stock will increase.

CONCLUSION:

I can give you lots of helpful advice, but none is perfect.

As beneficial as using common sense. Have faith in your data, and never lose sight of the supply and demand indicators equation.

As I said in trading psychology, you need to master your setup. It would be ideal if you chose your trading approach independently. When I use the word "attack," I mean it in the broadest sense possible because many of the tools we employ have characteristics in common with opposing warring armies. You must provide an answer to where you will feel most comfortable and how you will fight the battle, much like a general planning strategy before the conflict. It would be better if you understand your personality to decide what you are most suited for in the industry. You might feel most comfortable working as a short-term equity trader.

I prefer to approach the market like an investor. However, do not forget that many other options are available to you, even though I often talk about stocks.

You have the freedom to choose because the technological concepts we have studied apply to all market places and are simply transferable between the various fields. Moreover, the Indian market has significantly matured over the past few decades. As a result, possibilities that had never been accessible to novice investors now have enormous potential.

Being involved in too many markets that trade differently from one another can be a problem caused by the availability of products. In certain professions, being a jack-of-all-trades and a master-of-none can be acceptable, but in this one, you should be aware of your limitations. For example, if someone, naturally an investor, tried to become a day trader, it would be like asking a freshwater fish to swim in the ocean. Consider your professional decision as a result.

Aapke bhai ki advice

Pehley paper trade kr k strategy ka back test karey.

After selecting a region, you must choose the appropriate instruments to achieve your objectives. It would be helpful if you practiced with all the technical tools and indicators using paper trades before you entered the market for the first time. Give the tools a chance, but make many little mistakes on paper. Trying each item out, at least initially, is the best method to decide which one you want.

When you invest your money in stocks or index options, you pay close attention to the charts and supply/demand patterns. Trust me on this.

Like all has its manzil, this journey of technical analysis also. I wish for your profitable trading Journey.

In case of any problem, Your brother is just a call away.

You may reach me anytime through my social media handler.

Mr. Mukul Agrawal Author